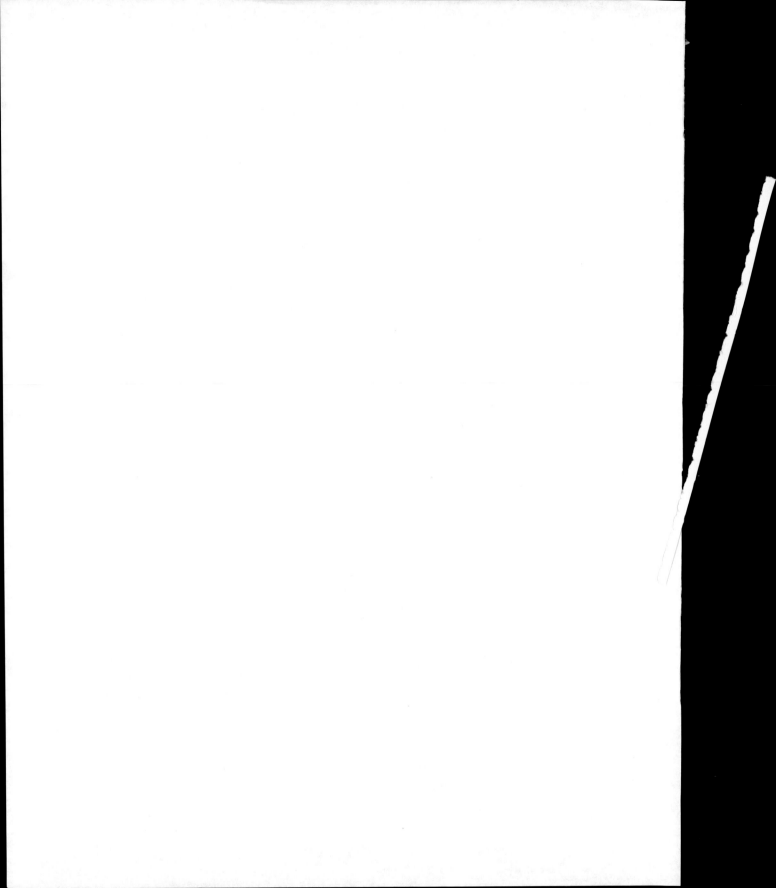

MAKING A Difference IN OUR FATHER'S HOUSE

The History of Trinity Missionary Baptist Church

BERNICE EATON and
Rev. Dr. GREGORY E. MOORE

ARCHWAY PUBLISHING

Archway Publishing books may be ordered through booksellers or by contacting:

Archway Publishing
1663 Liberty Drive
Bloomington, IN 47403
www.archwaypublishing.com
844-669-3957

ISBN: 978-1-4808-9604-8 (sc)
ISBN: 978-1-4808-9605-5 (e)

Library of Congress Control Number: 2020917998

Print information available on the last page.

Archway Publishing rev. date: 10/15/2020

CONTENTS

ACKNOWLEDGMENTS

Inspiration

My husband, David Eaton, and children, David II, Deidre, and Darryl
Reverend Dr. Gregory E. Moore, pastor, Trinity Missionary Baptist Church
Dr. Helen Louise Moore
Dr. Donnie Bellamy, retired professor, head of Social Science Department, Fort
Valley State University
Trinity Baptist church members

Special Recognition

Angeola J. Arnold
Lillian Kimbro
Ossie Lindsey
Alma Simmons
Brenda Weatherspoon
H. A. Hunt Memorial Library, Fort Valley State University
Special Collection, Washington Public Library, Macon, Georgia

Interviewees

William Arnold
W. S. M. Banks
Ernestine Barnette
Mamie Booth
Willie Brown

Daisy Canady
Marie Canady Cleveland
Dorothy Coleman
Isaac Crumbly
Alice Davis
Willie (Bo) Davis
Martin Edwards
Hattie Floyd
Mary Julia Marshall
William D. Moorehead
Willie D. Moorehead
Louise Rouse
Louise Young Sanders

Photography

Isaac Smith
Arthur Gibson

Editors

Dr. Anna Holloway
William Moore, photo editor

INTRODUCTION

History reveals that many of our African American churches emerged after slavery. Trinity Baptist Church's beginning was not until 1912, forty-seven years after slavery ended. Its heritage had its beginning from the Shiloh Baptist Church, its mother church. Shiloh Baptist Church, in Fort Valley, Georgia, began to form before slavery was abolished, when a small group of blacks in Houston County—now Peach County, Georgia—began meeting under a brush arbor to sing and to praise the Lord our God. As we sing the song "Steal Away" ("Steal Away to Jesus"), we can visualize the slaves creeping through the night into the deepest part of the woods, where their masters could not hear them. The book titled *Ain't Gonna Lay My 'Ligion Down*, edited by Alonzo Johnson and Paul Jersild, (Columbia: University of South Carolina Press), explained it best when it told how slaves entered into the woods out of hearing distance to sing, pray, preach, testify, and plan their escape.

During this period of slavery, some of the questions confronting Christian slave owners were as follows: "Should slaves be converted to Christianity?" and "Do they have a right to religion?" The rights for slaves became a controversial issue politically and religiously in both the North and the South. Politically, the slave had no rights. Religious leaders debated the interpretation of the Bible concerning slavery, each using it for their own advantage. Some resisted believing the slaves would see themselves as being spiritually equal. Others were persuaded that allowing conversion would work to make an obedient slave. As these attitudes changed, more opportunities appeared for evangelizing and providing religious instruction for slaves. The differences in values and viewpoints caused many of these denominations to organize their own regional associations to reflect their beliefs.

In 1845, it was noted in *Profiles of Black Georgia Baptists*, by Clarence Wagner (Atlanta: Bennett Brothers Printing Company), that a well-known Ebenezer Baptist Association appointed a committee to consider educating their slaves to Christianity.

The association represented several counties: Jones, Baldwin, Washington, Johnson, Laurens, Bleckley, Peach, Bibb, Twiggs, and Wilkinson. Although Peach was listed among the counties, Peach County emerged from Macon and Houston Counties in 1924. The association encouraged these slave owners to have their slaves confess to Christianity and attend their church. While some openly conducted religious meetings among the slaves, the owners typically suppressed their Christian faith. The association decided that all ministers should set aside a time to give special religious instructions to the slaves belonging to their congregation. Many of the slaves were converted and became members of the churches of their master; some became deacons and were assigned to other slave members, and others were called to preach.

Following the Emancipation Proclamation, according to Eric Foner's 1988 book, *America's Unfinished Revolution, 1863–1877* (New York: Harper and Row), the black pastors and laypeople began organizing their own association around 1868. Blacks worked together and combined their meager resources to purchase land and build their own churches. They formed their own associations and ordained their own preachers. By the end of the reconstruction period, a large number of churches and associations were organized in the South. One organization was the Middle Georgia Missionary Baptist Association. It later became a member of the General Missionary Baptist Convention of Georgia, Inc., and the National Baptist Convention, USA, Inc.

The Shiloh Baptist Church dates back to slavery and the Civil War. It began its worship services in 1863 at a place known as Union Hill. It was from this church that our own Trinity Baptist Church was born in 1912.

> *And so were the churches established in the faith, and increased in number daily* (Acts 16:5 KJV).

Although Trinity Baptist Church, being among the younger churches of Fort Valley, cannot boast of its connection with slavery, it has a rich and unique history of its own. Throughout its history, the members demonstrated their faith, their hope, and their courage as they went about doing God's will in making a better community for the people of Fort Valley and Peach County. Beginning with the founders of Trinity and continuing throughout its history, the impact of three pastors stood out among others. The first pastor, Reverend Cyrus S. Wilkins, was an active member of the Missionary Baptist Convention, where he served as vice president and interim president prior to accepting the leadership role at Trinity. He organized and named the church Trinity Baptist Church.

Reverend John L. Walker, the eleventh pastor of Trinity, served from 1929 through 1946. He was recognized for the completion of the church sanctuary. He was also responsible for planning and developing a proposal to include local college student participation within the church. This program, with the assistance of Dr. Horace M. Bond, president, Fort Valley State College (now Fort Valley State University), was extended to include all community churches.

Reverend Julius C. Simmons, the sixteenth pastor, served for forty-two years in the academic arena as well as pastor of Trinity Baptist Church. Reverend Simmons was an advocate for human rights and contributed to much of the progress made in Fort Valley and Peach County during the civil rights movement. By this time, the church was the central focal point in black communities. Trinity's annex became a meeting place to many local organizations. Trinity became known as the People's Church.

It has taken many years of research, slowly gathering bits of information from written and oral resources, to piece some of the history together. Documentation has come from many scattered sources: financial records, the first warranty deed, programs, conference minutes, minute books, newspaper articles, correspondence, written and oral histories, books, manuscripts, and census records. The unpublished manuscript papers of Fort Valley State College President Horace Mann Bond, Hunt Memorial Library, Fort Valley State University, and Fort Valley provided information about Trinity during J. L. Walker's administration at Trinity. The correspondence between Bond and Walker documented the beginning of faculty/student attendance and service within the community churches. This educational environment, along with having the college president and his family in attendance, began to influence many of the local youths to prepare themselves for college attendance. The Reverend Julius C. Simmons collection, 1958–1999, in the Trinity Baptist Church Archive, Fort Valley, documented changes in the physical appearance of the church through several renovations, as well as Simmons's involvement with local organizations. Organizations like the Citizens Educational Commission (CEC) and the Fort Valley Ministerial Alliance played an active leadership role resulting in many political and economic changes in Peach County.

The later part of this history gives credit to Reverend Dr. Gregory E. Moore, co-author. He wrote chapter 8 and "Pastor's Pen," nine through twenty-two. He had the courage to build a "bigger boat" to bring more people to Christ. The new sanctuary was completed in 2016. *Pastor's Pen* gives an update to the continued progress of Trinity.

Addendum to the Introduction
Pastor Gregory E. Moore, coauthor

At the writing of this history of Trinity Baptist Church, the current pastor is Reverend Gregory E. Moore, who has served from 2001 to the present. In his fifteen years of service, many new ministries have been birthed, including Seasoned Saints, noonday and evening Wednesday Bible study, Bible teacher training, new member orientation, men's retreats, women's retreats, youth retreats, a finance ministry, children's church, a gospel choir, new musical instruments, community outreach picnic, security ministry, praise team, dance team, mime team, the purchase of a new bus, and the construction of a four-hundred-seat sanctuary completed in January 2016. In addition to sanctuary space, the new sanctuary also includes a choir room, pastor and secretary office, nursery, a lounge area, a larger foyer, and a breezeway into the old sanctuary. The former sanctuary is slated to become a much larger fellowship hall. The multipurpose space and the former fellowship hall will be used as a space for kids' ministry.

Under Pastor Moore's leadership, a number of dilapidated buildings and houses around the church were purchased and torn down, making State University Drive, on which the church sits, more aesthetically pleasing to the eye. Many people in the community expressed gratitude to the Trinity membership for cleaning up a sizable area in the neighborhood

This brings the introduction of Trinity Baptist Church's 105 years of history to its current date. In the words of the great gospel singer Andre Crouch, "Through it all, through it all, we've learned to trust in Jesus, we've learned to trust in God." The Trinity membership gives all the credit and praise to the Lord, who has blessed them to be a church family for 105 years.

Chapter 1

THE FOUNDERS OF TRINITY BAPTIST CHURCH

Examine yourselves to see if your faith is really genuine.

—2 Corinthians 13:5 NLT

In the beginning, thirty-five individuals separated from their present church and started on a journey to create a new church. This journey, filled with faith, hope, and courage, led them to believe that they could make a difference in their community in Fort Valley, Georgia. Their meetings were conducted at the community's Mutual Aid Benefit Lodge Hall on the corner of Spruce and Pine Street under the leadership of the following deacons: Edward (Ed) Dawson, Tom Slappey, Charles Toomer, Robert T. Anderson, Oliver Manuel, and John Fuller.

Fort Valley is in Peach County, Georgia. It is located in the central part of the state. It is known for its peach industry, the Blue Bird Bus Company, and the historically black Fort Valley State University, founded in 1895.

These working-class individuals made a decent living working on the railroad, the Fort Valley lumberyard, peach farms, and as domestic workers. Fannie Nix and Charles Toomer operated their own businesses. Nix, a teacher, taught school from her home, and Charles Toomer operated a grocery store called the Tin House. He was also the owner of the Toomer Funeral Home in Fort Valley.

Their focus was to search for a strong spiritual leader. Reverend Cyrus S. Wilkins became the first pastor. He organized the body of believers and named the church Trinity Baptist in January 1912.

The church, founded on Christian principles, began its mission to help others know Christ through preaching and teaching His Word. Its missionary outreach began by bringing children to Sunday school to learn about God's Word, become good citizens, and reach out to others.

Alphabetically listed, the founders were Robert Anderson, Rosa Anderson, Mrs. Armstrong, Reverend Armstrong, William Belt, Clara Canady, Clark Canady, Anna Dawson, Edward Dawson, Bertha Emanuel, Carl Emanuel, Dye Felder, Julius Felder, Lelia Felder, Sallie Ford, Annie Fuller, John Fuller, Annie Lou Canady Armstrong Gray, Avan F. Jones, George Jones, Rosa Jones, Oliver Manuel, Beulah McIntyre, Lillie B. Felder Miller, Alfred Mitchell, Mattie Mitchell, Maude Polk Thomas Morgan, Fannie Nix, Henry Nix, Tom Slappey, Patience Thomas, Charles Toomer, Julia Wynn, Arthur Young, and Cora Young. These individuals shaped the future of Trinity.

Chapter 2

TRINITY BAPTIST CHURCH

…Upon this rock I will build my church.

—Matthew 16:18 NLT

Trinity Baptist Church was organized in January of 1912. Its existence as a church depended on the leadership of seventeen ministers who served as pastors from 1912 to the present. The remarkable leadership of three pastors—Cyrus S. Wilkins, John L. Walker, and Julius C. Simmons—stood out in shaping Trinity Baptist Church. Reverend Cyrus S. Wilkins, the first pastor, was from Columbus, Georgia. Reverend Wilkins was a member of the Missionary Baptist Convention. He served as vice president and later as interim president of the Missionary Baptist Convention in Georgia. He completed the term vacated by the well-known Reverend Emanuel K. Love, who died on August 24, 1900. Reverend Wilkins provided a sense of direction for the congregation. He named the church Trinity Baptist. It was not until 1971 that an application was submitted to the secretary of state for the official name to be incorporated. Today, except for public record, its members refer to the name as Trinity Missionary Baptist Church to emphasize its missionary work. Services for the newly organized church were conducted in the Mutual Aid Benefit Lodge Hall, owned by Gideon Barnette, located on the corner of Spruce and Pine Street, Fort Valley, Georgia. It was here that the members began to make plans for building a church.

Others followed Reverend Wilkins during the period from 1914 through 1929. No dates were located on their length of service. Reverend Franklin served as its second pastor. He implemented the building plans and instructed the trustees to begin the negotiations for purchasing property. A warranty deed signed by trustees R. T. Anderson, E. D. Dawson, and Tom Slappey, dated April 11, 1914, Houston County Courthouse in Perry, Georgia, recorded the purchase of two lots from E. M. Fagan for $219. This property, located on what was known as the Old Marshallville Road, became the permanent residence of Trinity Baptist Church. The Old Marshallville Road later became South Macon Street. Today the site is referred to as 505 State University Drive.

Reverend S. M. Hawkins, the third pastor, began the construction of a brick building. The work progressed slowly under the succeeding men: Reverend N. B. Wright, C. W. Warren, James R. Carter, E. D. White, Reverend Saxon, H. F. Taylor, and W. J. Reynolds.

It was not until the arrival of Reverend John L. Walker in 1929 that the building was completed and the congregation began to grow. He was the church's eleventh pastor. He resided at 306 Fourth Avenue, Macon, Georgia. He later moved to Fort Valley, to the Habersham building. Upon his arrival at Trinity, Reverend Walker was confronted with a large wooden structure that had sawdust floors and crude, hard, uncomfortable slat benches. He brought with him a vision for the completion of the building. He added the brick structure, completed the twin towers, and provided the wooden flooring, doing much of the work himself. He built two adjacent rooms for Sunday school classes. Funding for the later project was donated by Reverend Marion Daniel Reed, pastor of the First Baptist Church, Fort Valley, Georgia. Reverend Reed, having recognized Reverend Walker for his energetic ability in completing the building, provided funds through a cooperative agreement between the Southern Baptist Convention's Home Mission Board and the Executive Committee of the Georgia Baptist Convention to complete the annex.

Church, 1929

Reverend Walker was also recognized for designing a religious program for the college students attending Fort Valley State College, Fort Valley, Georgia. This program was the beginning of a college community relationship that changed the image of the congregation.

Trinity experienced a period of uncertainty when bringing in new ministers. The tenures were short-lived for some: Reverend Gaston Johnson Hubert (1946–1948),

Reverend Joseph E. Tackett (1949–1951), and Reverend E. F. Ridley (1952–1953). At the beginning of his tenure, Reverend Ridley organized a women's ministry called the Vigilante Club in 1952. Its purpose was to improve the appearance of the sanctuary and make it a beautiful place to worship. It continues today as Sisterhood of Dorcas. Reverend William Smith (1953–1957) served for four years.

Reverend Julius Caesar Simmons, (1957–1999), the sixteenth pastor, served for forty-two years. Simmons was recognized for many contributions at Trinity and his leadership within the community. He was responsible for improvements in both the interior and exterior of the church prior to 1976 and again in 1982, when the church was condemned due to storm damage. He also left a legacy of fighting against injustice adhered to by segregation in Fort Valley. Political and economic

1984.

issues concerning Fort Valley and Peach County were discussed through forums and brought to the attention of the people. Trinity became known as the People's Church. In recognition of his contribution to the city of Fort Valley, the council voted to name a street Julius C. Simmons in his honor.

Reverend Gregory E. Moore, the seventeenth pastor, who began in 2002, continues preparing the way for Trinity Missionary Baptist Church, taking it into the next century. Today's additions to the church include a church steeple, a new heating/air-conditioning unit, and a bigger marquee built to house the original bell removed from the bell tower. Reverend Moore's vision has included building a new sanctuary and an expansion of the existing building to include a children's church.

Chapter 3

THE REVEREND JOHN L. WALKER YEARS, 1929–1946

Faith without works is dead.

—James 2:26 NKJV

Let your light so shine before men, that they may see your good works, and glorify your Father, which is in heaven.

—Matthew 5:16 KJV

The fond memories of Reverend John L. Walker (1929–1946) still echo among the senior members of the church who recall his seventeen years as pastor of Trinity Baptist Church. Reverend Walker came to Macon, Georgia, from Alabama, his home state. He was a graduate of Alabama Baptist University, Montgomery, Alabama; Tuskegee Institute, Tuskegee, Alabama; and the State Normal School for Teachers, Montgomery, Alabama. He was a teacher in the Eastman public school system, Eastman, Georgia.

Having accepted the position as pastor at Trinity Baptist Church, Reverend Walker was immediately confronted with financial problems. The church had an outstanding debt of $900.40. Adding to this problem was an unfinished church building. However, he found a dedicated membership willing to work. Reverend Walker's ideas, skills, and his energetic working capacity resulted in the accomplishment of completing the church building and the elimination of the debt. The church conducted its dedication cornerstone service on October 6, 1929.

> *For we are his workmanship, created in Christ Jesus unto good works, which God hath before ordained that we should walk in them* (Ephesians 2:10 KJV).

Trinity's Sunday services and activities were scheduled to begin with Sunday school at 10:00 a.m., junior church at 11:15 a.m., and morning worship at 11:30 a.m. The afternoon and evening auxiliary meetings included missions at 4:00 p.m., willing workers mission at 5:00 p.m., training union at 7:00 p.m., and ended with the evening worship service at 8:00 p.m. Some of the church officers serving under Reverend Walker who have been verified include Deacon Martin Edwards, chairperson, board of deacons (1941)and Sunday school superintendent (1938–1944); Deacon Dennis Clark, church clerk (1942); Deacon A. Arrant, financial secretary; Cornelius V. Troup, chairperson, board of trustees; Julia Edwards, treasurer (1942); Rose Isom, pianist; and Ophelia Roberson, chairperson of the Deaconess Board.

Reverend Walker played a key role in changing the image of Trinity. According to tradition, the Fort Valley State College family differentiated itself from the locals in the community. Walker's religious program resulted in the beginning of an interaction between the students with community church activities. Fort Valley State College, having an emphasis on teacher education, was relatively new as a four-year state school. Dr. Horace Mann Bond became its first president (1939–1945). Trinity planned a special college day program for students on November 19, 1939. Its objective was to bring together the school officials, students, and church folk, and to stimulate an interest of goodwill. Dr. Bond was invited as guest speaker. Reverend Walker was impressed. Their relation-

Fundraising Activity

ship with each other grew. On several occasions, Walker requested assistance from the Bond family during church activities. To emphasize their friendship, one such incident appeared when Walker requested President Bond's help during an upcoming revival. In a letter dated April 1, 1941, Walker wrote, "I am trying to find places for dinner each day for Reverend I. S. Powell, First Baptist Church, Bainbridge, Georgia, who is our revivalist. I am asking you to please help by preparing a dinner on Wednesday, May 7, at your home. If you can arrange this, please let me know by this weekend." Another friend was Reverend Marian D. Reed, pastor of, First Baptist Church. He consulted with both individuals on many occasions for educational advice, spiritual insight, and support. The two men inspired Walker by accepting his idea.

> *You must teach these things and encourage your people.*
> ––Titus 2:15 (NLT)

Christian Advance through Church School

"Christian Advance through Church School" was a program designed to extend religious and educational interaction among students through attendance and participation in the church's activities. Dr. Bond was strongly in favor of this proposal, especially with the college's emphasis on teacher education. In critiquing the proposal, his conclusion was that it would not only allow the prospective teachers to teach the children in the rural communities but also, through volunteer service, give them the opportunity to observe and become knowledgeable of the family life, existing health, and education background of individuals living in the area.

Reverend Reed's review focused on another perspective—that of developing leadership skills for the students. His vision was for students to have regular attendance in Sunday school and church activities at Trinity and be involved in cooperative programs offered to colleges and universities by the Southern Baptist Convention. The First Baptist Church held membership with the Southern Baptist Convention. He explained how Mercer University, Macon, Georgia, participated through its Baptist Student Union. The religious affiliation provided by the churches, plus workshop experiences at the convention, would not only make them knowledgeable but also would give them the skills needed to work with individual groups within the communities.

The college family was desirous of maintaining a functional relationship with the community's religious institutions. The administration believed that this relationship would stimulate goodwill among the church people, school officials, and students. Dr. Bond encouraged the students, along with the faculty and staff, to participate in the work of the churches throughout the Fort Valley community. He taught a young men's Bible class at Trinity.

The Southern Baptists Convention provided funds to Trinity for the students to attend the annual convention. Reverend Walker worked diligently with the students and their involvement with the educational programs. He became affiliated with the beginning of The First Baptist Youth Conference for Baptist Negro Students in Georgia, which was organized in 1941. He assisted Dr. D. B. Nicholson, secretary, Baptist Student Union of Georgia, in planning the student activities for its first annual conference. Reverend Reed and the First Baptist Church provided the social activities and refreshments, and Trinity's choir provided the music. Vashti Walden, a member of Trinity, was elected to serve as chairperson of the Committee on Arrangements and charged with the preparation for the second annual conference to be held February 20–22, 1942.

Trinity Baptist Church was the host church for the third annual conference, February 26–28, 1943. This conference was cosponsored by the Baptist Student Union of Mercer University and the Baptist Student Union of Georgia. The theme of the conference was "Working Together with Christ." One of the highlights of the session was a discussion on "present-day problems, which are perplexing youth." A roundtable talk session on race relations was conducted by Dr. C. L. Jordan. The conference leaders in attendance included Dr. D. B. Nicholson, secretary, Baptist Student Union of Georgia; Reverend M. D. Reed, pastor, First Baptist Church, Fort Valley; Reverend W. W. Weatherspoon, executive secretary of Missionary Baptist Convention, Atlanta; and Mrs. L. L. Craig, director of Young People's Work, National Baptist Convention, Atlanta, Georgia.

Reverend Walker's work with youths was known throughout Middle Georgia. He served as president of the Middle Georgia Baptist Youth People's Union (BYPU) Convention and as a member on the BYPU executive board.

Reverend Walker found time to attend workshops offered by the Macon Rural Institute, sponsored by the Home Missions Councils. Reverend V. A. Edwards, a religious extension worker, was director, representing six central Georgia counties: Lamar, Monroe, Crawford, Peach, Bibb, and Macon. The annual rural leadership institute was designed for "colored" ministers. Its focus was on present conditions and possible improvements in relation to family life, education, and the health and welfare of the rural churches. The Georgia Baptist College, Macon, Georgia, served as host for its annual sessions held on May 26–30, 1941. Workshops and evening sessions were conducted at local churches. Walker participated in one of the sessions with a message called "God's Acre Plan."

Reverend Walker was an active participant with The Fort Valley Ministerial Alliance. This organization addressed many community problems in Fort Valley. They considered solutions and made decisions based on the best approach or option in solving these concerns. He served as vice president along with other officers: A. Bell, president; Roy Moore, secretary; and H. K. Sanders, parliamentarian, 1943.

Tenth Anniversary Celebration

Reverend Walker's success at Trinity was expressed during a special celebration for his tenth anniversary. The congregation, community churches, and pastors throughout Fort Valley and Middle Georgia participated in a twofold weeklong celebration for his tenth anniversary as well as the church's twenty-seventh anniversary (1939). Churches were invited to participate in the program. A message was delivered each night. The participating churches were Reverend C. B. Batts, Central Union Baptist Church, who spoke on Wednesday night, substituting for Reverend Wilder. The Central Union usherette board sponsored a program for Thursday night, with Reverend I. E. Evans delivering the message. Reverend L. A. Calhoun, Shiloh Baptist Church, delivered the message on Friday night, sponsored by its BYPU. The Sunday morning worship service was conducted by Reverend V. G. Stallworth and his church in Perry, Georgia. Reverend B. L. Richburg and Reverend A. Glawson, New Hope Baptist Church, Macon, Georgia, ended the celebration with afternoon messages.

Resignation

Church Officers, 1942

The membership of Trinity grew to more than two hundred members under Reverend Walker's leadership. Student attendance was very good. Each Sunday a parade of students from the FVSC campus would walk to the local churches in Fort Valley. Several families connected with the college joined Trinity and began to serve in the activities. Reverend Walker and his devoted wife, Emma, loved Trinity, and its members loved them. Emma, by profession, was a practical nurse. She worked with the adult choir, the Sunbeams youth choir, and served as a primary class Sunday school teacher.

Reverend Walker retired from Trinity Baptist Church in 1946. He continued his career as a teacher at the Dodge

County public school system, Eastman, Georgia. He enjoyed working with students. He was a humble, approachable individual. Valeria McCrary, a member of Trinity, told of her experience with Reverend Walker. This was the beginning of her 1947 freshman year at Fort Valley State College. She needed a ride to the campus. Her parents asked Reverend Walker if he would assist by letting her ride with him to Fort Valley. She recalled his kindness and concern for others. He treated her as if she were his own child. He not only drove to the college; he made sure she was checked into to the girl's dormitory and assigned to her room before leaving.

Reverend Walker returned to Trinity to preach the installation sermon for his replacement, Reverend Gaston Johnson Hubert. Trinity recognized Reverend J. L. Walker posthumously in 1973 and named its new multipurpose building the Anderson/ Walker Educational Annex.

Chapter 4

TRINITY'S PASTORS, 1946-1957

Reverend Gaston Johnson Hubert, married to Julia M. Hubert, served from 1946–1948. He was installed as Pastor of Trinity Baptist Church on July 1, 1946. He came from Tremont Temple Baptist Church in Macon, Georgia. Deacon Martin Edwards met him at the association and was instrumental in getting him to come to Trinity. His tenure at Trinity was short-lived. He later resigned, returned to Macon, Georgia, and began serving at the Union Baptist Church, Macon, Georgia.

Reverend Joseph E. Tackett served from 1949–1951, preceding Reverend Hubert. His wife was Marnesba Tillman Tackett. She was an English instructor at Fort Valley State College. Rosa Evans, one of the older members, joined Trinity under his leadership. Ernest Corker and Luetta McCrary, both Fort Valley State College students, began worshipping at Trinity under Reverend Tackett's leadership.

Reverend Walter R. McCall served as interim pastor February 1952. Reverend McCall served as dean of men and director of religious activities, Fort Valley State College, Fort Valley, Georgia.

Reverend E. F. Ridley served from 1952–1953. He was a native of Macon, Georgia. He graduated from Morris Brown College and did further study at Atlanta University; the Interdenominational Theology Seminary, Atlanta, Georgia; and the University of Omaha in Omaha, Nebraska. Reverend Ridley was responsible for organizing a women's ministry. He gave it the name Vigilante Club in September 1952. Today it is known as the Sisterhood of Dorcas Ministry.

Reverend William Smith served from 1953–1957. He became Trinity's fifteenth pastor. Reverend Smith was born in Hickman, Kentucky. He received a bachelor of science degree from Drake University, Des Moines, Iowa, and a bachelor of divinity and master of theology from Crozier Theological Seminary, Chester, Pennsylvania. He came to Fort Valley from Philadelphia, Pennsylvania, with his wife, Inez Jane Wallace, and six children—Wilmetta Ann (Langston), Theresa Inezene (Jenning), William Amos, Jr., Martin Andrew Robert, John Alden, and Henry Allen. He was employed

Reverend William A. Smith
1954–1957

William Smith

at Fort Valley State College as associate professor of education and director of religious activities. Dr. C. V. Troup, president of Fort Valley State College and chairperson of the board of trustees, Trinity Baptist Church, was instrumental in offering him the position as pastor of Trinity Baptist Church. His wife, Inez Smith, accepted a position at the college as secretary under Dr. Marian Myles, head of the Department of Mathematics and Science. She later served as secretary at H. A. Hunt High School, under Professor Henry E. Bryant, principal.

William D. Moorehead, a longtime member of Trinity, came to Fort Valley State College as a professor in biology in 1954 and joined during Reverend Smith's tenure. He observed Reverend Smith as "a unique stately man" who conducted his sermons in a timely manner. He recalled that the worship service began promptly at eleven o'clock and lasted for one hour. His sermon was fifteen to twenty minutes. Earnest Corker, a student at Fort Valley State College in the early fifties, remembered Reverend Smith also as an excellent speaker. Reverend Smith was recognized for reviving the Fort Valley Ministerial Alliance and beginning an annual Christmas project to help a needy family during the holiday. Reverend Smith resigned in September 1957 after accepting a position as director of religious life and dean of men at Fort Normal and Industrial Memorial College, St. Augustine, Florida.

Chapter 5

THE REVEREND JULIUS CAESAR SIMMONS, 1957–1999

All who listen to my instructions and follow are wise.

––Matthew 7:24 LB

Matthew 7:24 teaches that practicing obedience to God's Word becomes the solid foundation to weather the storms of life. To follow God's instructions, one must be a hearing and a responding disciple.

Reverend Julius Caesar Simmons (1957–1999), a native of New Rochelle, New York, was Trinity Baptist Church's sixteenth pastor. Reverend Simmons succeeded Reverend William Smith in November. He received AB and master of divinity degrees from Virginia Union University, Richmond, Virginia, and did postgraduate work at the Fort Valley State College (now University), Fort Valley, Georgia, in the field of guidance and counseling. He was married to Alma Alexander. They have two children, Patricia Diane and Julius C. Simmons, Jr.

J.C. Simmons

Reverend Simmons left a legacy affecting many who encountered him as an administrator/teacher/counselor in the academic environment, as a minister through religious affiliations, and as a minister/advocate in the Fort Valley community.

In the academic environment, Reverend Simmons served Fort Valley State College as dean of men, director of religious activities, counselor, and director of financial aid. As dean of men and director of religious activities, he had the opportunity to interact with students and become their trusted mentor and counselor. Jeanes Hall was a residence for male students and for the Simmons family. He was a compassionate person who understood and worked diligently for the success of his students. One of his many

J.C. Simmons Family

students was Reverend Winfred Hope. While a student at Fort Valley State College, Hope received ministerial experiences serving under Reverend Simmons as assistant pastor of Trinity Baptist Church, 1965–1966. Reverend Dr. Winfred Hope matriculated from Fort Valley State College, completed his ministry degree, and became a well-known pastor of the Ebenezer Baptist Church West, Athens, Georgia. As director of financial aid, Reverend Simmons also helped students who were struggling financially receive aid in order to complete their education. He retired from Fort Valley State University in 1991.

Reverend Simmons came to Fort Valley as a young minister and a servant of God, taking on a big responsibility. He began to put into action what he had studied in seminary school. He humbly accepted the word that God had planted in his heart as a message to obey and practice. Trinity Baptist was Reverend Simmons's first church. His Christian leadership and administration were driven by a team effort, with the support of seasoned deacons led by Martin Edwards, chairperson of the board of deacons. Other staunch and faithful officers of the church were: Benjamin Anderson, Sunday school superintendent; Dr. Cornelius V. Troup, chairperson, board of trustees; Dr. W. S. M. Banks, financial secretary; Dr. O. E. Hicks, clerk; and McKinley Wilson, treasurer.

He served as a distinguished minister and was recognized as a community leader. He had a deep voice that demanded attention when he delivered his message in a lecture style or spoke at public gatherings as moderator. He conducted revivals, appeared on numerous programs at the college, and was invited as guest speaker during many of the black high school baccalaureate and commencement exercises. Reverend Simmons was an advocate for justice. His northern background did not hinder him when discussing racial issues and problems existing in the South. He believed in justice for all when it came to the rights of people. He reached out to blacks and whites, adults and children, educated and uneducated, both individually and collectively. From the pulpit, he repeated the message of injustices in Fort Valley frequently to his congregation as he spoke of the "colored only" and "whites only" signs located at downtown drinking fountains. To receive service at the one and only fast-food restaurant, blacks had to go to the side of the building labeled "colored only." He expressed his concern for people traveling on the highways to and from the South and having no public restrooms or hotel facilities available for "colored." He befriended the homeless living on the streets. He invited them to attend church. One or two visited Trinity at various times. There were not as many as we have today. One individual, referred to as "Goatman," liked Reverend Simmons and called him "a good man." Reverend Simmons sympathized with domestic workers who had worked for white families all their adult lives with no means of financial benefits or support, with old age meaning they could no longer work. He talked about the unfair practice of downtown businesses, expressing concern that some businesses had all-black clientele, yet the only blacks hired were janitors. There were no black clerks at these businesses.

He was a man of action when confronted with unfair injustice. He did not back away when an issue needed to be resolved. William D. Moorehead, a member who served Trinity for over fifty years, described him as "a man of character and courage." It took courage that could have affected his life in protecting one of his members. The incident happened before integration at the Peach County Hospital in the late 1950s, as told by Moorehead, where his first child was prematurely born. Their family doctor wanted the mother to be close to the nursery; therefore, his wife was placed in a nonsegregated room.

The doctor was a highly respected individual at the hospital and in the community. He was among the two or three individuals who lived on "the other side of the tracks" and attended programs at the college. He perhaps did not think of the repercussions the incident might have caused; even though segregated laws were gradually being abolished in the South, the hospital rooms remained segregated.

Both he and Reverend Simmons were concerned for the safety of his wife being left alone through the night. Reverend Simmons made the decision that he stay during the night, and luckily, it was without incident. According to Moorehead, his wife, Willie D. Moorehead, became the first black to integrate the Peach County Hospital in 1958.

Reverend Simmons spoke up for his family in another incident recalled by his daughter Patricia Diane (Stuckey). Patricia Diane was admitted to the same Peach County Hospital for surgery. A room was not available in the segregated ward; therefore, she had to wait in bed in the hallway. Reverend Simmons asked why she could not be placed in the section where rooms and beds were available. She was later moved to the nonsegregated area without incident. According to Patricia Diane, she was the first to integrate the hospital. The two incidents were perhaps months apart, which the writer did not question. The same doctor was involved in both incidents. Several years later, in 1965, Reverend Simmons became the first black asked to serve on the Peach County Hospital Authority Board. He was nominated to serve as chairperson in March 1980.

Reverend Simmons served as a consultant for a group of black students at the recently integrated Fort Valley High School who, on their own initiative, staged a demonstration by walking out of the classrooms in protest against what they believed to be unfair treatment of black students. To break up the crowd at the school, the students reported that officials at the school had sprayed them with mace. Patricia Simmons and Ronald McCrary, along with other students, brought their complaint to Reverend Simmons. Having heard their complaint, he counseled them and asked them to return to the school. After contacting the principal with a follow-up appointment, the incident was resolved. The students were allowed to return to their classroom with no further incidents.

Renovations of Trinity Baptist Church

Reverend Simmons led the congregation through two renovation projects as well as a crisis that almost divided its membership. The church's appearance had remained the same over its many years of existence. He guided the congregation into an agreement to improve both the exterior and interior of the church. Its first renovation began in 1960 with the appointment of the General Building Fund Committee. Daisy Lewis served as chairperson. In a memo dated November 29, 1960, Lewis requested that each committee member make a report of the money raised. In 1961, the sanctuary was completely renovated and decorated with new furniture and pews.

In 1966 and again in 1968, the trustees, having been instructed to purchase land for future expansion, purchased the connecting properties surrounding Trinity as land became available. The land at the side of Trinity was property owned by the late Mrs. Henrietta Walden Myers, a former home economics teacher at the college. The Henrietta Walden Myers Home Economics Building at Fort Valley State University is named in her honor. With the purchase of this land, the church was able to provide ample space to build a new unattached annex. Groundbreaking ceremonies for the annex were in 1972. The Anderson/Walker building was completed in 1973, with space available for parking. In 1975, there was the addition of a vestibule, new restrooms, a roof over the two towers, and the original brick of the exterior was painted white.

This new design gave the building a new look. It completely changed the appearance from a plain building into a beautiful white brick contemporary structure. A rededication celebration was held on March 28, 1976. The sanctuary was filled to capacity by worshippers who gathered on a Sunday afternoon to hear a message delivered by former Fort Valley State College President Dr. Cornelius V. Troup, Sr. (1946–1966) of Atlanta, Georgia. Dr. Troup served as a member of Trinity from 1938–1966. Many came to hear Dr. Troup's message and to fellowship with coworkers, former students, and others in attendance, such as Dr. Waldo W. E. Blanchet (FVSU president, 1966–1973) and Dr. Cleveland W. Pettigrew (FVSU president, 1973–1978. It was during Dr. Troup's tenure as chairperson of the board of trustees that the original plans for the renovation of the church's sanctuary and the construction of an educational building (annex) were formulated.

The second renovation came with an unexpected message concerning the condition of the church due to a storm. Reverend Simmons announced that the church had been badly damaged. The storm damage to the roof had caused the infrastructure to weaken. This was verified with an inspection and ruled by the county inspector that it could no longer be used for service. It had to be vacated.

Trinity was faced with a difficult decision that would have a tremendous impact on the unity of the congregation. The church's conference minutes reveal that Reverend J. C. Simmons and Elijah Weatherspoon, who succeeded Martin Edwards as chairperson of the deacon board (1981), proceeded to lead a divided congregation through this difficult period. Trinity's future was at stake. Half of the congregation wanted to build a new church, while the other half wanted to repair the church sanctuary by replacing the damaged roof and walls. Money became an issue since no preparation had been made toward building a church. Several intense and sometimes heated discussions took place before coming to an agreement. The impact of Trinity's small membership weighed heavily on the direction to be taken. Though the walls crumbled, Reverend Simmons's leadership kept the congregation together through prayer and by following God's instructions through his Word. A decision was made, with everyone agreeing to repair the sanctuary.

To weather the storms of life, we must practice being obedient to God and let him take control. The renovation of the building began with the appointment of Philip Brewton as chairperson of the building committee. The members were Jacquelyn Demons, vice-chairperson; Evelyn McCray, secretary; Sidney Hand, Darold McCrary,

Clifford Ponder, and John Moody. Their assignment was to work with the architect and the John Pitts Construction Company contractor.

Worship services continued each Sunday in the educational annex while the work progressed. St Peters AME and Usher's Temple CME Church gave permission to use their facility for special services and events. With the completion of the new building, additional improvements were made by joining the unattached educational annex to the sanctuary, adding handicap accessibility. The pews were also refurbished before returning to the sanctuary. The congregation returned to a beautifully decorated sanctuary on March 18, 1984, having a much stronger faith and a deeper commitment to doing God's will.

Community Outreach

Historians tell us that great men and women have nurtured an outreach commitment to do well unto all men through the years by having a strong faith in God and an unselfish desire to give of themselves to serve the Lord. The black clergy, minister, and pastor became the prime leaders of black communities nationwide, not only in religious matters but also in reaching out into secular spheres of politics, economics, education, and sociocultural activities. This too can be witnessed during the leadership of Reverend Simmons at Trinity. He took the lead as he treaded untouched waters of injustices adhered to by segregation in Fort Valley as well as the state of Georgia. He opened the doors of Trinity for organizations to conduct weekly and monthly meetings in the Anderson/Walker annex. Important political and economic issues were discussed through public forums and brought to the attention of the people through these organizations.

On October 15, 1969, a community-wide protest moratorium was held at Trinity. Reverend Simmons worked diligently through the Fort Valley Ministerial Alliance with other ministers, the Citizenship Education Commission, and the National Association for the Advancement of Colored People (NAACP) to keep the public informed on current issues of race relations statewide and nationally. Reverend Simmons voiced his concern about the importance of voting at a National Association for the Advancement of Colored People (NAACP) program on June 27, 1976. During his remarks, he explained that the destiny of the nation, the state of Georgia, the county of Peach, and the city of Fort Valley rested in the hands of the registered voter who exercised his opportunities to cast his vote in the various elections. He strongly urged the audience not to allow the destiny of others to be affected because you did not do your civic duty.

An outstanding church member and community leader, Deacon Claybon J. Edwards, son of the late Deacon Martin Edwards, referred to Reverend Simmons as "the glue" that held the black community together because people listened to him and sought him for counseling and advice.

Trinity was sometimes referred to as the educated church. It was also known near and far as the People's Church. Its community outreach assisted in Trinity wearing this label. When asked how we adopted the slogan the "People's Church," Reverend Julius Caesar Simmons answered that the membership's arms were always open to welcome those who cross the threshold. "Our doors are open to worshippers who wish to stop and share Christ with us."

The Fort Valley Ministerial Alliance

The Fort Valley Ministerial Alliance was an organization of black ministers. Reverend Morris Hillsman, pastor of Shiloh Baptist Church, Fort Valley, Georgia, was its president in 1983, when the Fort Valley Ministerial Alliance contributed to a boycott against the Revco Drug Store called "Operation CURE." The July 21, 1983, issue of the *Macon Telegraph* cited "Revco Becomes Target of a Black Boycott." It appeared that two white men allegedly manhandled a pregnant young black woman accused of shoplifting. Neither the sheriff deputies nor the Revco personnel found any evidence on the woman. After pursuing negotiation for a settlement, Operation CURE went forward and organized a picket line in an effort to boycott the Revco store in Fort Valley.

Reverend Simmons presided over many meetings held at Trinity Baptist Church. He informed an audience of approximately fifty persons of issues addressed with the executives from the Revco Drug Centers, Inc., Twinsburg, Ohio, to remedy the problem. The two issues addressed were (1) to dismiss the clerk and pharmacist involved in the incident, and (2) to hire more black managers and a black pharmacist. The Revco Drug Centers executives refused to negotiate. Reverend Simmons expressed concern that this was not the first incident and that they were there tonight announcing that they would not be treated as others would treat us. Many supported the cause by taking their business to other stores in Fort Valley. As a result, the Revco store lost business.

Recognition for Service and Leadership

Reverend Simmons was recognized locally and statewide for leadership, service, and contributions to the Fort Valley community. A local individual referred to the church as a missionary outpost under his leadership, officially recognized by the Georgia Baptist Convention, through annual financial grants, and for the high quality of service it rendered to and through the young people attending there.

Letters of congratulations were received on Trinity's sixty-eighth church anniversary from the Honorable Jimmy Carter, president of the United States of America, Washington, DC. President Carter wrote the following: "Rosalynn and I are pleased to send our best wishes to each of you and to join in your prayers for continued blessings on your congregation and on our nation."

The Honorable Herman E. Talmadge, United States senator, Washington, DC, also extended his congratulations in a message: "This is certainly a memorable milestone for Trinity Baptist Church, and I know you are very proud. I have always felt a special fondness for the members of Trinity Baptist Church, and I commend each of you on the spiritual guidance and influence you have shown in your community." The Honorable George Busbee, Office of the Governor, Atlanta, Georgia, sent greetings with these words: "The history of Trinity Baptist Church is marked by the loyal and dedicated service of its members. You can take pride in the knowledge that you are continuing the tradition of this Christian institution that has so enriched the community of Fort Valley."

An invitation was given to Reverend Simmons by the Honorable Thomas B. Murphy, congressional representative and Speaker, House of Representatives, Atlanta, Georgia, to serve as chaplain of the House of Representatives on Friday, March 2, 1979, via request of the Honorable Bryant Culpepper, Fort Valley, Georgia. The Honorable Paul Reehling, who served five terms as mayor of the city of Fort Valley, said, "Thanks to strong and dedicated

Reverend Julius C. Simmons at the State Legislative, Atlanta, Georgia, 1979. L-R: The Honorable Bryant Culpepper, Reverend Julius C. Simmons, The Honorable Thomas B. Murphy, Speaker, House of Representatives

leadership, Trinity Baptist Church has been a focal point, a great meeting place, a forum of ideas, and even, at times, a political force."

The Honorable Rudolph J. Carson, mayor of the City of Fort Valley commented, "Not only have you contributed so much to the religious and spiritual life of this community, but you have [also] been the focal point for social and civic concern and action in this community. You have fulfilled your mission as a full-service institution, making available your facilities and resources for the total development of the individual and the betterment of the entire community."

The Fort Valley City Council voted in March 2000 to rename Alabama Street to J. C. Simmons Street in honor of the late Reverend Julius C. Simmons. The ceremony was followed by a reception at Trinity Baptist.

Reverend Simmons served on the Countywide Voter Registration Committee, Christmas Stocking Fund, Fort Valley Evening Optimist Club, Emanuel Bible College, Thursday Night Ministers Class, Prison Ministry, the Union Baptist Missionary and Educational Association of Middle Georgia, Congress of Christian Education, and the National Baptist Convention. He served as commencement and baccalaureate speaker at numerous high schools throughout middle Georgia: Jeffersonville High School, Jeffersonville, Georgia, 1958, A.M. Fields, principal; The Houston High School, Perry, Georgia, 1965, J.R. Hightower, principal; Risley High School, Brunswick, Georgia, 1966, J.S. Wilkerson, principal; and A.S. Staley High School, Americus, Georgia, 1968, Daniel L. DeLoach, principal, to name a few. Business and government officials consulted him frequently regarding matters of paramount importance to the entire Middle Georgia community.

Although Reverend Simmons departed this life before entering the new millennium, Trinity shall be ever reminded of his powerful messages as he envisioned God's work and the future of Trinity Baptist Church. We were reminded of things that happened in the past and what we must look forward to in the next century by working diligently and cooperatively to make Fort Valley a better community. Sharing with others was important. This was predicated upon the idea that we will share with others what we have: our material means, our friendship, our goodwill, our hope, our love, our undaunted faith in God, and our faith in the possibilities of all God's children. We believe that the ongoing mission of Trinity and true religion are to keep at work rebuilding and redeeming society, dealing justly with our fellow men, and walking humbly with our God.

Chapter 6

A CONGREGATION OF BELIEVERS

For it is God who is at work in you.

—Philippians 2:13 (NASB)

Paul reminds us that we are all members of one body working together for Christ Jesus, who is the head of the church. United as one, believers must have faith in Jesus Christ and be committed to serve Him and to do His will according to His purpose (Romans 12:5 KJV).

The new church, knowing the value of an education, began its long journey in making a difference in the community. This journey was based on their Christian faith –– trusting God to lead them; their hope, full of expectations; and their courage to persevere on this course of action.

The congregation, having a select group of thirty-five individuals and their families, began its worship services. This group envisioned having a new church that would be "representative of its membership," having a common background instilled with characteristics of good morals and values. The heads of household may be described as working skilled and unskilled laborers according to the US Census. Many were homeowners. Their wish seemed no different from others seeking a better way of life and opportunities for their family. Their mission was to serve God and use their talents to reach out to others in need.

Living in the South produced many challenges for people of color—economically, educationally, politically, and socially. A high rate of illiteracy existed in Georgia. This was especially true for the black population in Peach County as well as many other surrounding small cities where unemployment fluctuated. Employment was at its highest during the peach season, when menial or unskilled jobs were plentiful.

Educating the minds of children was important to Fannie Nix, one of the founders. She was a teacher. Fannie and Henry Nix opened their home on South Macon Street (Tyson House) to teach children in the community basic education (reading, writing, arithmetic).

During personal interviews with two well-known native citizens of Fort Valley, Willie (Bo) Davis, Central Union Baptist Church, and Mamie Booth, both talked about the limited educational opportunities for children in Peach County. According to Davis, only a few parents could afford tuition to attend the Fort Valley High and Industrial School. This institution, located in Peach County, was a private institution founded in 1895. The tuition fee at the Nix school was ten cents each week. Andrew Booth, husband of Mamie Booth, and Willie Davis attended the Nix School. Davis felt that the Nix school gave him the opportunity to get an education.

Both began attending school after Nix moved it from her home to a building on Wye Street. This one-room building was located near the railroad tracks. In order to heat the building, the boys were given the responsibility of picking up coal that had fallen from the boxcars along the tracks. It was after moving to Trinity's church that the Nix school began its first commencement and school closing program. Davis completed grades one through eight and later enrolled in the Fort Valley High and Industrial School.

A new public elementary school for "colored" opened in 1928. This building, called the Training School was located on South Macon Street facing the Fort Valley High and Industrial School. Dorothy Colemen, St Luke Episcopal Church, Fort Valley, Georgia, and Lois Fluellen Jones were teachers assigned to the first-grade class at Trinity Baptist Church. According to Dorothy Coleman, Trinity's classrooms were used by the school as an extension for the first-grade student overflow.

Growth in the Church

The work of the church was an inspirational experience for its founders as well as for second-generation individuals like Lessie Felton Davis, Blanche Clark, and Loisteen Morgan Smith, who followed the example of their parents. They took the lead among others and worked diligently in the church as well as the community. Lessie Felton Davis served in the Sunday school, the choir, and any other capacity where she was needed. She was an active member of the parent-teacher association (PTA), serving as president. Blanche Clark and Loistine Morgan Smith became Sunday school teachers. Smith served as president of the missionary and worked with youth activities.

Children from the communities who attended Sunday school were taught to read, sing, pray, and participate in church activities. It was the beginning of an education process for some and for others the only schooling they would receive. The Bible, used as a textbook, taught the children to memorize Bible verses. The church leaders visited the communities to encourage parents to let their children attend Sunday school. Rosa, wife of Robert Anderson, was successful in bringing children from the Gano community. On Sunday morning, the children were ready, excited, and waiting for their teacher to arrive and take them to Trinity. Angeola Jackson (Arnold) loved to tell the story of how her parents agreed to let her and her brother attend Sunday school. She explained that her parents were Primitive Baptists and their church did not have Sunday school. She was the youngest among the group; therefore, Mrs. Anderson held her hand as they walked down South Macon Street to Trinity. It was with hope that the children would grow up in the church and go on to become adult leaders in life. This was the beginning of Angeola's Christian journey at Trinity.

Angeola Jackson (Arnold), a native Fort Valleyan, attended Trinity most of her life, beginning in Sunday school at the early age of five or six years old. She joined Trinity as a teenager during a revival, along with her friends Elizabeth Maddox and Johnnie C. Davis, son of Alice Davis. The three were baptized at the Shiloh Baptist Church on the fourth Sunday in April 1929. Angeola remembered Shiloh as the only black church in Fort Valley with an indoor pool. Martin and Julia Edwards were also baptized. Angeola served for over seventy-five years.

She participated in Sunday school and choir, and she was a deaconess, an usher, a member of the Vigilante Club, and a devout missionary worker in the Women's Missionary Society. She was a great fundraiser for the church and served on numerous committees, working beside others like Alice Davis, Julia Edwards, Annie Gray, Mary Lyons, Annie Porter, Hattie Floyd, Felma McCrary, Alberta Rumph, and Doris Lavender, to name a few.

She completed her education at Fort Valley State College. She taught in the Peach County public school system. She enjoyed teaching her social studies classes by adding local history. Her love for history inspired her to write an article about her church titled

"Trinity as I Knew It," which was published in the local *Fort Valley Leader Tribune* newspaper.

Trinity attracted others who migrated to Peach County, for one reason or another, from surrounding counties: Alice Davis (Ross), Martin and Julia Edwards, Mary Frances Davis Lyons, and William Arnold, to name a few. Alice Davis was a teenager when she and her parents moved to Fort Valley. Reverend C. W. Warren, her stepfather, was pastor. She did not remember the dates but believed it to be between 1915 and 1919. She joined under Reverend C. W. Warren. She spent several years of her young adult life in Detroit, Michigan, before returning to Fort Valley. She became an active missionary member. The church surprised her with a one hundredth birthday party celebration on January 17, 2000.

Martin Edwards, a lifelong resident of Middle Georgia, was born in Macon County and reared in Taylor County. He moved to Fort Valley in 1920, shortly after wedding Julia Mitchell in 1919. He was employed at the Kell Grocery Warehouse in Fort Valley as a deliveryman. Edwards established the Fort Valley Undertaking Company, which grew tremendously and later became known as the C. J. Edwards Funeral Home when his son took over the business. He and his wife, Julia, reared two sons and five daughters.

He and his wife gave their lives to Christ under the leadership of Reverend J. L. Walker. They were baptized at Trinity in 1929. He was ordained as a deacon and served thereafter as chairperson of the board of deacons.

Approximately six years after their golden wedding anniversary, Sister Julia passed away. He later met Rilla King and joined in holy matrimony. She stood close by his side, giving strong support to his Christian endeavors.

He was a member of the board of trustees and superintendent of the Sunday school. The Union Baptist Missionary and Educational Association of Middle Georgia, Inc., of which Trinity Baptist Church is a member, recognized his leadership ability and talent when they elected him to serve on the executive board and as treasurer of the Laymen's Auxiliary.

Julia Mitchell Edwards, the wife of Martin Edwards, was a native of Taylor County. While rearing seven children—Hazel, Eloise, Mary Julia, Mildred, Rose, Andrew (AJ), and Claybon—Julia Edwards took care of her religious affiliation at the church. She served as church clerk, treasurer, chairperson of the building fund committee, member of the willing workers mission, cochairperson of the under-shepherd group, member of the Women's Missionary Society, Vigilante Club, and deaconess. She was a Good Samaritan who reached out to the sick, helping wherever needed if it meant transporting individuals to and from the doctor or hospital. Her son Andrew and daughter Mary Julia continued at Trinity. Claybon served in the US Army, moved to Detroit, Michigan, and later returned after the death of his brother to help his father with the business.

Mary Frances Davis Lyons moved to Fort Valley from Houston County. She moved her membership to Trinity under the pastorate of Reverend J. L. Walker and began singing in the choir, serving as an usher, and joining the Women's Missionary Society. Sister Lyons was honored for fifty or more years of service to Trinity. She was the aunt of Evelyn Davis McCray. She reared Evelyn and her four brothers—Calvin, Earnest, Johnny, and Rudolph—bringing them up in Trinity after the loss of their mother.

William Arnold came to Fort Valley as a student and graduated from the Fort Valley Normal and Industrial Institute, a two-year institution. In 1938, it became a state college known as Fort Valley State College. It was here that he met and married Angeola Jackson in 1941 before being called to serve in the United States Army during World War II. He joined Trinity and served with his devoted wife for more than sixty years. He was ordained along with Chester Wilkerson, another college graduate, as deacons under the leadership of Reverend Julius C. Simmons in 1960. He was a member of the board of trustees.

Sunday School Superintendents (1912–1944)

Trinity was blessed to have the strong leadership of four individuals who gave more than a total of thirty years of service as Sunday school superintendents. Robert Anderson was the first superintendent. He was one of the three trustees who signed the deed to purchase the church property. He was given the responsibility of the overall organization of Trinity's Sunday school in 1912. The classes under his supervision were the Lelia Felder primary class, the Pearl Underwood junior boys' and girls' class, and the Nettie Byrd intermediate class. The Surluker (also spelled Zaluka) Holmes adult class was named for the first African American woman pharmacist in Fort Valley. Dr. Surluker (Zaluka) Holmes operated a drugstore in the Vineville community. Dr. H. A. Holmes and his family moved to Fort Valley in 1915. His medical practice was in Fort Valley. They resided with their five children on South Macon Street.

The Sunday school classes were scattered throughout the sanctuary. The primary class was located near the woodburning stove to keep the little children warm. Deacon

Robert Anderson was married to Rosa Anderson. The US Census records, 1920, listed him as a laborer employed at a lumberyard (Freight Depot, Fort Valley).

Deacon Alfred (Al) Mitchell was the second superintendent. He was listed in the US Census records, 1920, as a bricklayer.

Dr. Walter T. Ford succeeded Mitchell. Dr. Ford, a dentist, was a native Fort Valleyan. He may have followed Dr. Marlow, who was perhaps the first black dentist in Fort Valley. Walter Ford was a young adult when he and his siblings began attending the new church with their mother, Sallie, one of the founders. He graduated from Fort Valley High and Industrial School in 1913. Ford completed his degree in dentistry and returned to Fort Valley to practice. His office was located on Church Street downtown. Angeola Jackson (Arnold) served as secretary for both men. Dr. Ford also taught the adult Bible class. He died in 1946.

Deacon Martin Edwards (1900–1988) served as the fourth superintendent, circa 1938–1944. Some of the officers assisting him were Deacon Dennis Clark, assistant superintendent; Eloise Edwards, secretary; Ruth L. Lawson, assistant secretary; and Sister Winn (Wynn), treasurer. By this time, according to a 1938 minute book, a standard Sunday school program was followed. Sunday school began at the ten o'clock hour each Sunday morning with an opening song, followed by prayer, scripture, and the devotional thought. The superintendent set the tone by introducing the lesson and the reading of scripture passages in unison. On cue, a musical rendition was a signal to the students to stand and prepare themselves to march to their appropriate classes. A flag bearer carried the Christian flag. Connie Troup, son of Dr. and Mrs. C. V. Troup was recorded as one of the flag bearers. The classes were taught for thirty-five minutes before reassembling with the superintendent. Each class reported to the secretary the number in attendance and the amount of money collected. The superintendent closed by giving a review of the lesson, followed by the secretary's summary report and the closing song before dismissal.

The classes were taught by Miss Loestine Morgan (Pearl Underwood class); Miss Blanche Clark, (Nettie Byrd class); Mrs. Bessie Stamps, (Lelia Felder class), and Reverend J. L. Walker (Surluker Holmes class). Sometimes the classes were combined and taught by the superintendent or Reverend Richburg, a local minister who attended Trinity. A list of student names recorded from a 1938 minute book included Dorothy Brown, Rebecca Davis, Mary Julia Edwards, Mildred Edwards, Eloise Edwards, Miss Smith, Miss Brown, Miss Richman, Dorothy Wright, Johnny Livnion, Perty Mae Brown, Miss Gate, Inez Harris, Andrew Maddox, Lillie Mae Hill, Frankie Junior Hill,

Robert Lee Hill, James Henry Town, Berk Simpson, Hattie Humphry, Lois Batts, Ruth Lawson, Rebecca Davis, and Rosina McCrary.

Reorganization of the Sunday School Classes

The importance of Sunday school and youth attendance was one of the highlights of Reverend Walker's administration. Reverend Walker extended a cordial welcome to the students and faculty that came from Fort Valley State College, H. A. Hunt High School, and Fort Valley Training School. Cornelius V. Troup and W. S. M. Banks began church attendance at Trinity shortly after their arrival at the college. Banks became teacher for the adult class. The name of this class became the W. S. M. Banks adult class. Troup was later asked to teach the young women from the college. This class was given the name of its first teacher and became known as the C. V. Troup collegiate class. Ozias Pearson, dean of men, continued teaching this class after Dr. Troup retired in 1966. Miss Alee James, instructor of home economics, was appointed assistant to W. S. M. Banks's adult class.

The adult Bible class, taught by Dr. Walter T. Ford, a local dentist, remained the same. Three classes, the intermediate, junior boys, and junior girls were added. Walker appointed additional staff to include Mrs. Bessie M. Stamps, vice president, parent-teacher association, intermediate class; Mr. R. L. Williams, H. A. Hunt High School teacher, junior boys' classes; and Mr. Gamaiel Hilson, an FVSC student, junior girls' classes. He began a training program and appointed Mr. A. Arrant, a retired postal service worker, as director of training. A training union was established for college students. Miss Mary Julia Edwards (Marshall), an FVSC student, was appointed director.

Sunday School Superintendents (1945*–2015)

During the period 1945 through 2015, five individuals served in this position as Sunday school superintendent: Benjamin S. Anderson, Vincent Murphy, Wilmetta Langston, Douglas Moorehead, and Alfred Conteh.

Benjamin S. Anderson relocated to Fort Valley, Georgia, in 1945 from Alabama, as agriculture professor at Fort Valley State College. *The date he was appointed superintendent is unknown. Brother Ben, as he was called, worked diligently, encouraging the students and transporting them to Sunday school. Anderson also served as chairperson of the board of trustees, 1966–1971. He was an active participant with the Citizenship Education Commission (CEC). He married Lula Mae Sutton, who preceded him in death in 1955. They had a son, Benjamin, Jr.

Vincent Murphy accepted the position of superintendent in December 1967. He came to Fort Valley from Alabama in 1961 to work for the city of Fort Valley as a police officer. He was later employed by Fort Valley State College in the Department of Plant Operations. Murphy and his wife, Carrie, became active members of Trinity. He immediately became involved with Sunday school and was appointed assistant superintendent in July 1961. Yvonne Beauford served as secretary. Murphy served on the board of deacons as secretary. The Murphys reared three sons: Vincent, Jr., Llewelyn, and Melvin. He supported the youths by participating with the community baseball team and Boy Scout Troop 245, sponsored by the church. Madie Cornelious (1969–1974), Elijah Weatherspoon (1975–1978), and Wilmetta Langston (1979–1989) served as assistants during his tenure.

His wife, Carrie, served as a deaconess, missionary, and member of the Vigilante Club. Murphy passed away unexpectedly in 1989. He was honored posthumously during Trinity's one hundredth church anniversary for services rendered at Trinity and the community of Fort Valley. Two of his sons, Llewelyn and Melvin, were in attendance to see the unveiling of their father's portrait. Murphy's portrait is currently housed in the Anderson/Walker Annex with other dedicated men of Trinity: W. S. M. Banks, C. V. Troup, Benjamin Anderson, Martin Edwards, and Pastors J. L. Walker, William Smith, and Julius C. Simmons.

Wilmetta S. Langston became the first woman at Trinity to serve as superintendent of the Sunday school. She was appointed superintendent upon the death of Vincent Murphy in 1989 and again in 1999, as assistant superintendent under Douglas Moorehead. Langston was a teacher/librarian for forty-plus years and helped with planning and directing the Sunday school programs, along with Wilma J. Anderson and Madie Cornelious. She expressed how pleased she was when asked to plan and direct her first annual Christmas program in 1960.

Wilmetta Smith (Langston) joined Trinity in 1954 under the leadership of her father, Reverend William A. Smith, pastor. She came to Fort Valley with her parents, Reverend William A. and Inez Smith, and four siblings. Having transferred from Temple University, Philadelphia, Pennsylvania, to Fort Valley State College during the spring quarter, she and her siblings experienced culture shock in Fort Valley. At the age of eighteen, she joined the United States Army, Women's Division, 1957–1960, before returning to Fort Valley State College to complete her education. She accepted a position as secretary under Daisy Lewis, itinerant teacher trainee, vocational home economics. At Trinity, she met and married Charles Langston. They have a son, Charles "Chuck" Langston, Jr. She retired from the Houston County public school system, Perry, Georgia.

Langston served on many of the auxiliaries (now referred to as ministries) at Trinity. She held many of the elected positions in the Sisterhood of Dorcas and Chancel Choir. She served as advisor on youth programs—vacation Bible school, Katye Troup Ushers, Baptist Youth Fellowship (BYF), and Baptist Training Union. She chartered the first Girl Scout Brownie Troop for black girls in Fort Valley in 1968. She served on the board for the Girl Scout Council of Middle Georgia and as a leader for the Boy Scout Council of Central Georgia. In 2015, she became a member of the trustee board.

Douglas (Doug) Moorehead, Jr., was appointed Sunday school superintendent in 1999. He served in this capacity from 1999 to 2004 and was appointed again by Reverend Gregory E. Moore in 2016. He grew up in Fort Valley and joined Trinity at an early age. In keeping with a family tradition, his grandfather, Reverend W. A. White, Alexander, Louisiana, baptized him. Douglas was active in the children's choir, vacation Bible school, Sunday school, as an usher, and in other youth activities. As an adult, he continues to serve where needed, as an usher, ambassador, assistant Sunday school superintendent, and adult Sunday school teacher. He was ordained as a deacon in 2012 under the leadership of Reverend Gregory E. Moore.

Alfred Conteh served as Sunday school superintendent 2005–2015 under Reverend Gregory E. Moore. Alfred Conteh was born in Sierra Leone, Africa. He moved to Fort Valley, Georgia, and later joined Trinity in 1986. He was ordained as a deacon in 1992, under the leadership of Reverend Julius Simmons. He teaches the adult class. He is the father of twins, Alfred and Alvin, who grew up in Trinity.

The Annual Sunday School Picnic

There were joyous activities for the young as well as the old. Each year the community churches gathered to fellowship at the annual Sunday school picnic. They gathered at a place called John Millers woods, located on Scuffletown Road, the southernmost part of Carver Drive. Mr. Miller was overseer on the J. H. Beard farm, and the yearly picnics were held on his property. These local churches fellowshipped and celebrated the goodness of God, allowing Him to fill them with joy.

> *Go and celebrate with a feast of choice foods and sweet drink, and share*
> *gifts of food with people who have nothing prepared.*

>   ––Nehemiah 8:10 KJV

John Effie, Friendship Baptist Church, would always beat the drum, and the youngsters would strut and march, keeping step with the music. Each church would furnish its own food, but all of the churches would contribute equally to pay for the lemonade for everyone. The churches continued in later years, with individual picnics at Camp John Hope, Fort Valley, Georgia.

A Traditional Change: The College Impact at Trinity

The impact that the college family had at Trinity resulted in a gradual change prior to the 1960s. Traditionally, the congregation in general included local folk, families who lived on South Macon and Pine Street, as well as the Gano, Griffin Line, and Vineville communities.

This overall transition took place during the administration of Dr. C. V. Troup, president, Fort Valley State College, and Reverend Julius C. Simmons, pastor. Dr. Troup—along with his wife, Katye, and sons, Cornelius, Jr., Elliot, and Kenneth—came to Fort Valley from Brunswick, Georgia, in 1939. Dr. Troup succeeded Dr. Horace Mann Bond in 1945. He continued to perpetuate Bond's idea of faculty and student involvement in the local churches. At Trinity, he taught a Sunday school class and served as chairperson on the board of trustees. As president at the college and chairperson of the trustees at Trinity, he was in a position to offer Reverend William Smith the position of assistant professor of education at the college and the position of pastor that was available at Trinity Baptist Church. He repeated a similar dual position offer with Reverend Julius C. Simmons, who replaced Reverend Smith at Trinity. William Arnold, a trustee, stated it best when he said, "He was everybody's boss, and they followed what he suggested." Dr. Troup gave twenty-seven years of service to Trinity. He was credited for the early planning stages of Trinity's renovations.

Several individuals within the congregation who migrated to the college in the forties had already begun to make an impact at Trinity. Dr. W. S. M. Banks, a college professor, and his wife Hattie, were among the early individuals who brought about a change at Trinity. He came from Mississippi and met his wife, Hattie, at Fort Valley State College. He joined the faculty as a social science instructor under the leadership of Dr. Horace Mann Bond. Banks served as a Sunday school teacher for over thirty years, with only a break to serve his country in World War II, where he rose to the rank of captain, and to pursue his doctoral degree. The adult class was named in his honor as the W. S. M. Banks adult class. He served as a church officer on the board of trustees, assistant superintendent, financial secretary, and on numerous committees. Banks was active with the Citizenship Education Commission (CEC). This organization, although not a part of Trinity, paved the way for blacks in Peach County to enter into the governmental operations of politics. W. S. M. Banks became the first black to run for public office in Fort Valley. His wife, Hattie, and son, William Jr., also were active members of Trinity.

Henry Joyner, an agriculture professor at the college, was an adult Sunday school teacher at Trinity. Professor Joyner; his wife, Helen; and their children were among the early arrivals of faculty members attending Trinity. His children—Sandra, Eloise, and Gordan—grew up in Trinity. The Joyners later moved to Huntsville, Alabama. Attorney Gordan Joyner, son, continues to visit Trinity from Atlanta on special occasions. He kept in touch with Reverend Simmons and frequently supported the church with donations in honor of his parents.

Odess E. Hicks came to the college in 1947 as a French professor in the Foreign Language Department. He and his family joined Trinity and became faithful members. He and his wife served in the adult choir. He was later appointed church clerk, serving until his death in 1978. Dr. Hicks wrote our first record of the history of Trinity. His wife, Murlenum Hicks, a teacher in the Peach County public school system, served as pianist, organist (1966–1976), and choir director for the adult choir, which later was named Chancel Choir. Their daughters, Mariam and Carolyn, grew up in Trinity. Murlenum Hicks moved to California shortly after the death of her husband to live with her daughter Mariam.

Robert Church came to Peach County as an agricultural extension agent in 1948. In his work with rural blacks, he was able to improve the quality of life for poor farmers, teaching them the results of agricultural research in order to increase production. He continued the famous Ham & Egg Show that was originated in Fort Valley by the late O. S. O'Neal. Deacon Church came to Trinity from Athens, Georgia. He served over fifty years at Trinity, which included time spent as a church officer on the board of deacons, chairperson of the mission ministry, ambassador, fundraiser, and as a consultant offering his expertise on other committees. His public service work was extensive in the community. His great accomplishments included serving on the Fort Valley City Council, 1974–1982; spearheading the city's certification; and paving of streets and providing sidewalks in the black community. He served as a member on several boards. He served with Family and Children Services as a board member and as chairperson for fifteen years. His wife, Ruby, and two children, Robert, Jr., and Annette, were members of the St Luke Episcopal Church. They also attended Trinity to give support as a family.

McKinley Wilson, another product of the 1940s, served as church treasurer and on the board of trustees. He was employed by the Georgia Department of Education in the Division of Vocational and Agricultural Education, which was housed on the Fort Valley State College campus. He was executive secretary to the state's New Farmers of America Association and director of Camp John Hope FFA – FCCLA Center. He came to Fort Valley in 1947. His wife, Marsha, was a public school teacher. Their children, Barbara, Lois, and Charles, grew up in Trinity.

The college became a driving force that brought blacks to Fort Valley. Several factors contributed: an increase in the student population; additional faculty and staff employed; jobs became available in the newly integrated public school system; and better economic conditions opened up for African Americans. Many of the earlier families who migrated to Fort Valley via Fort Valley State College had become permanent residents as well as active members within the community churches. There was also an overflow of student attendance each Sunday. This higher level of education brought about new ideas and challenges within the churches. Trinity continued to focus on programs to attract youths as well as adults by providing educational, social, and cultural events for the community.

Visionary Community Outreach Leaders

Trinity's congregation was known to reach out into the black community. Houston Stallworth was a man of vision when he supported the cause for education, the church, and the community. He came to Fort Valley in 1945 as professor of Horticulture and Plant Science at Fort Valley State College. He later was appointed chairperson of the Division of Agriculture. He served on numerous organizations as a board member and president of Peach County Improvement Association as well as on state committees. He did agriculture research missions in Hawaii, Haiti, and Puerto Rico.

Houston Stallworth, like the founders of Trinity, had a vision to make a difference in the community of Fort Valley. The Citizenship Education Commission (CEC) was organized when he, along with other individuals, discussed having better living conditions and opportunities for blacks in Peach County. Dr. Stallworth was elected president. The purpose of CEC was to inform and get citizens of Peach County involved in decision-making policies in government through voting practices. Although Trinity was not directly involved with CEC, Reverend Simmons supported the cause and opened Trinity's doors as a meeting place for local organizations.

Houston Stallworth

CEC addressed many of the concerns of the black community—voter education, registration, youth development, housing, employment, citizens' rights, political issues, and minority businesses. The impact of this organization influenced a number of Trinity's members as well as outside individuals to become involved in order to bring about change in policy-making decisions for the benefit of all people.

CEC became deeply engaged in a tremendous citizenship voter education registration project, August 9, 1964, in Peach County. Statistics from the Fort Valley voter registration office revealed that 4,500 blacks qualified to vote in Peach County but only 1,300 were registered. The goal of CEC was to secure as many of the remaining 3,200 potential black voters qualified before the deadline date. Its objective was to bring about a realization of a greater sense of civic pride and respectability on the part of more than 3,000 unregistered black citizens of Peach County.

One of the vital areas of service was CEC's Adult Education project. Training sites were set up throughout the black communities of Fort Valley and Byron in Peach County. Trinity became headquarters for the Trinity Baptist Citizenship School located in the church annex. This project was spearheaded by a team of teachers, local volunteer workers, PTA workers, and SCLC/SCOPE (Southern Christian Leadership Conference/Summer Community Organization and Political Education) workers. Mrs. Nella Crooks and Ida Miller served as cochairs with the following teachers: Wilma

Anderson, Hattie Banks, Freddie Gibson, Rosa Gilbert, Mrs. J. C. Lumpkin, Harriett Tabor, Annie Mae Porter, Nellie Bell Holsey, Ruth Troutman, Lessie Strickland, Gladys Grace, Mrs. Willie Ford, Marjorie Thorpe, Fozzie McMullen, Collen Williams, Mr. Cecil Porter, Miss Betty Martin, Freddy Gibson, and Glover Gibson. The PTA. workers were Annie Mae Porter, Mattie Dunn, Jessie Gross, and Miss Corine Gibson. Many of the volunteer teachers were from the Peach County school system. The SCOPE workers were student volunteers from the University of Minnesota who were willing to forego their vacations and summer jobs to give of their time and energies to meet the challenge.

Political education, voter registration, and literacy classes were taught at Mount Olive Church in the Vineville community, Trinity Baptist Church, Tabor Project Center, Central Union Baptist Church, and First-Born in the Gano community. The Trinity Baptist Citizenship School on South Macon Street served the Fagan Circle, Carver Drive, and Albany Railroad areas. Its purpose was to provide literacy training for prospective voters. These basic adult education classes were designed to educate people on how the political process worked. There were formal classroom settings as well as informal meetings held on the streets (one-on-one), rallies, and within the homes of local persons.

According to CEC, there is no record prior to 1964 of black individuals running for public office in Fort Valley. During the 1964 election, two individuals accepted the challenge. W. S. M. Banks became the first black candidate in Fort Valley to qualify for a position, and A. J. Edwards qualified as the second. In 1968, Benjamin Anderson led the race 687 to 640 for Fort Valley Council Post 4 against a white incumbent. The deciding vote went to a runoff. Support grew with the CEC organization as it politically educated people throughout Peach County about the power of voting. Many Peach County citizens began placing their names in the race for various offices. David Cornelius, also a member of Trinity, ran for the fourth district seat on the Peach County Board of Commissioners.

CEC reached out to help a group of 250-some white and black civil rights protesters marching for justice to the state capital in Atlanta. It solicited contributions to purchase food and provide a secure place for the night. The marchers began their march in Perry, Georgia, and arrived in Fort Valley on May 19, 1970, for their first stop. Hosea Williams, an official of the Southern Christian Leadership Conference (SCLC), led the march. They marched behind the wagon-drawn team of one white mule and one black mule as an exhibition to their protest of the brutal slaying of six youths by racist whites in the cities of Augusta, Georgia, Jackson, Mississippi, and Kent State University, Kent, Ohio. Three trucks followed, carrying coffins that represented the murdered victims. Trinity opened its doors as headquarters to the marchers. A rally was held on Tuesday night at Trinity, and the mixed group of whites and blacks remained overnight. College students and other youths joined the marchers. Businesses in downtown Fort Valley closed early, fearing that college students would become involved and riots would begin. Ossie Daniely Lindsey, a native Fort Valleyan, remembered playing cards with some of the marchers at a relative's house next door to Trinity. Ignoring a request from Governor Lester Maddox that the march should be called off, Hosea Williams and the group continued to the capitol building via Macon, Forsyth, and Griffin, Georgia, to meet with other demonstrators in Atlanta.

CEC invited Honorable Shirley Chisholm, US congressional representative from the Twelfth Congressional District, to Fort Valley as a featured speaker in 1976 for a political rally held in honor of D. L. Inman from Thomasville, Georgia. Inman was running for a seat on the Georgia Public Service Commission. Several Peach County candidates in the August primary were Dr. Houston Stallworth, Democratic candidate for county commissioner, and Albert (Al) Wilson, Republican candidate for sheriff. Congresswoman Chisholm expounded on the topic with a speech titled "What Do You People Want Now?" She spoke to an audience of over two hundred enthusiastic black and white individuals at Trinity Baptist Church. Congresswoman Chisholm, the first black female elected to the US House of Representatives, told the elated audience about blackness in all aspects of life in this country. Several local newspapers quoted Chisholm. "Blacks must be ready to struggle because that old spirit of racism still prevails on all of the country's governmental levels." Too many times when blacks have gone to places to receive that which was rightfully theirs, the question "What do you people want now?" was asked. She explained that the only desire of the black men in this country is to have their just share of the American Dream and that these powers that exist in the black community can be unlocked by way of the ever-powerful ballot box.

In 1970, Claybon J. Edward entered the arena of politics and became the first black to be elected to serve on the city council in Fort Valley. Claybon J. Edwards was born and reared on Pine Street, directly behind Trinity in Fort Valley. He and his siblings grew up in Trinity. Upon the fulfillment of his military duty, he found employment in Detroit, Michigan. He lived there for a number of years, until his father asked him to come home and help with the funeral home business. However, after winning the election in 1970, he was refused a position on the city council due to a disenfranchisement law. This disenfranchisement law was basically to keep blacks from running for public office. A suit followed and was taken to the US Federal District Court, Middle District of Georgia, Macon, Georgia, where a ruling was made by Judge Griffin Bell in the US Circuit Court of Appeals in favor of Edwards, declaring the city's voter purging effort unconstitutional. He was seated in 1971 as a member of the city council and later served as mayor pro tem under Mayor Paul Reeling.

Claybon; his wife, Mary; and daughter, Denise, continued to serve as faithful members at Trinity. His grandchildren, Sabastian, Samantha, Courtney, and Caitlin, also grew up in Trinity. He became a member of the board of trustees, chairperson of the mission ministry, an ambassador, and an ordained deacon. He served on numerous committee assignments. He was known throughout the state of Georgia for his involvement with business as well as politics. With all of his many accolades, he remained a humble servant, helping individuals not only at Trinity but also throughout the community of Fort Valley and Peach County.

Blacks turned out in record numbers for the 1980 election. The first black mayor of Fort Valley, Rudolph Carson, was elected. He was unseated in the 1982 election. Carson had served on the Fort Valley City Council as mayor pro tem since 1972, under Mayor Paul Reeling. He was a member of Central Union Baptist Church. Robert Church was his campaign manager.

The CEC was not only involved with governmental politics; it addressed an economic change in the hiring of blacks in businesses in Fort Valley for jobs other than those of custodial workers. Paulette McCray, daughter of Evelyn McCray, was the first black cashier hired at the A&P grocery store in Fort Valley.

Dr. Houston Stallworth died suddenly in 1978 without knowing the powerful impact and results this organization had on the citizens of Fort Valley and the state of Georgia.

Evelyn Davis McCray succeeded Stallworth. She became the first female president of CEC (Citizens Education Commission). She served for ten years in this position. McCray, a public school

Evelyn D. McCray

teacher/librarian, was another visionary and talented leader. She pursued her vision as cofounder of the Hunt Educational and Cultural Center (HECC) in 1980 with the late Professor H. E. Bryant, principal, H. A. Hunt High School. This black school existed prior to integration. Together they made the decision to rescue the beloved H.A Hunt High School gymnasium from abandonment and disrepair and preserve the building and its history by establishing a community center complex. With support from the community and the help of fundraising projects to purchase the land, the renovation of the building became a reality. In 1987, the Hunt Educational and Cultural Center was incorporated as a grassroots nonprofit organization and became a community center for youths and adults. The mortgage burning ceremony for the property was held in 1993.

In celebration of the twentieth anniversary of HECC in 2001, a bronze sculptured bust of Professor H. E. Bryant was unveiled. It was placed in a memorial garden along with a time capsule in honor of Professor Bryant for his many accomplishments as principal, assistant superintendent, and so forth, in Fort Valley, Georgia. Evelyn McCray did not stop with the additions of these projects. She continued working with public officials in the preservation of the H. A. Hunt High School auditorium. In 2009, the auditorium was named in honor of the late Anna L. Lumpkin, H. A. Hunt High School choir director. She also visualized the creation of a walking trail around the complex. Her most recent accomplishment was in 2015, when an official dedication of the walking trail was made by the Honorable Barbara B. Williams, mayor of Fort Valley, Georgia, and named the Evelyn Davis McCray Walking Trail in her honor.

She is still constantly setting new goals and standards as she brings others along to follow her example. Today her plans are twofold: (1) the inclusion of the community complex site on the National Register of Historic Places, and (2) the creation of a wall of history at the complex.

She moved to Fort Valley at an early age. She joined Trinity at the age of twelve and became actively involved in Sunday school, BYPU, Dorcas, Chancel Choir, and the building committee for the annex. She has been and continues to be involved in numerous community and state activities.

Her daughters, Gail, Jacqueline, Paulette, Avis, and Anita, grew up in Trinity. Anita; her husband, Richard Hogan; and their sons, Timothy, Jonathan, and Richard II, have continued as faithful members of Trinity. Anita serves as church treasurer.

Hattie Banks, a retired public school teacher, was founder of the Peach Area Professional Services (PAPS). She was instrumental in the opening of the Peach Area Professional Services building in November 1980. The mission of PAPS was to attract and encourage black professionals to practice in Fort Valley. The events leading to the dedication of the building began in 1977, when a group of concerned citizens decided something needed to be done about the small number of black professionals practicing in Fort Valley and Peach County. The group banded together under the leadership of Banks and set on the mission of building an office building on State College Drive, across from the college, to attract more minority professionals. Dr. James Jones was the only black medical doctor in Fort Valley at this time. Several professionals expressed interest and were contacted. Dr. Vincent Mallory, MD; Dr. Chester Little, DDS; and Gregory Homer, Attorney-at-Law, began practicing in Fort Valley.

Other PAPS officers who worked closely with Banks, who served as PAPS president, and to make this a reality, were Eugene Abrams, vice president; Gloria J. Street, secretary; Evelyn McCray, corresponding secretary; James McKeller, treasurer; and Dr. Melvin Walker, chairperson of the building committee.

Banks loved working with children and was active with Sunday school and vacation Bible school. She also served a term as president of the Vigilante Club. She was community oriented and was the first black woman to seek public office. Hattie Banks was the wife of Dr. W. S. M. Banks.

Isaac J. Crumbly organized the "Christmas Cheer Fund," which operated for over a period of ten years. He came to Fort Valley State College (FVSU) via way of Mississippi to teach biology. He and his wife, Dorothy, joined Trinity and became active in the community. They have two sons, Isaac Ooyiman and Konata Ato. While working with the community baseball team along with other members of Trinity, he had the opportunity to see some of the same poverty conditions in Georgia that he had witnessed in Mississippi. In an interview, Dr. Crumbly talked about seeing kids playing with cans for footballs, sticks for baseball bats, and stuffed socks for balls, and he said he decided that he could help make a difference by giving them a football, a bat, or a ball. This idea grew, with others joining. The purpose of the Christmas Cheer Fund was to solicit donations to purchase toys and distribute these items to local families in need. "Christmas Cheer," he said, "was very dear to my heart."

Isaac Crumbly

In 1972, during this period of unrest, Dr. Crumbly

ran for county commissioner while working with CEC. He also served as cochairperson with Thomas Dortch, a student at FVSC (now FVSU), with an organization called Citizens and Students for a Better Community (CASBC). Together they recruited students to assist in talking to people in the community about the importance of voting and helping people register.

Crumbly has continued using his talents to help others and has achieved success nationwide as a developer of innovative programs as a researcher, teacher, and mentor. In 1983, Crumbly received a small grant from the US Department of Energy (DOE). From this grant, he developed and founded the Fort Valley State University's Cooperative Developmental Energy Program (CDEP). This program has provided over a $30 million impact for the college and its students. Because of CDEP's dual degree programs, FVSU ranked number one in the nation for several years in graduating African Americans in mathematics and statistics. President Ronald Reagan recognized him in 1988 for exemplary achievements as an educator, researcher, and role model. He received President Barack Obama's 2009 Presidential Award for Excellence in Science, Mathematics, and Engineering Mentoring and was selected to President Barack Obama's PCAST Working Group on Science, Technology, Engineering, and Mathematics (STEM) Committee for Higher Education in 2011, along with receiving many other honors and awards.

Since 1992, CDEP has awarded over $12 million in scholarships to academically talented minority students throughout the United States. As of this writing, Courtney Small is the first CDEP scholarship recipient (2016) from Trinity. She is a freshman at FVSU, majoring in biology. According to Crumbly, Courtney has been invited to attend the University of Nevada in Las Vegas this summer, where she will be studying health and physics. Ikea Smith, another Trinity member, was awarded a 2017 CDEP scholarship to attend FVSU.

The Ambassador Ministry

A brotherhood of male members called the Ambassadors Club began in 1971. It observed its first Men's Day program during worship service on October 31, 1971. Previous Men's Day programs were held prior to this time, but not under the umbrella of the Ambassador Ministry. Alma Simmons was appointed by Reverend Julius Simmons to serve as program coordinator for beginning this occasion. Edward Dyson and Elijah Weatherspoon were cochairpersons. It was not until 1976 that several men saw the need to develop a more formal approach to the activities that would involve the men of the church. A constitution was written, stating that (1) the organization shall be known as the Ambassadors Club, and (2) the Ambassadors Club shall be to support the church activities in an organized manner, with emphasis on activities involving men and boys. The name was later changed to Ambassador Ministry, the purpose for them being to serve as mentors for the youth; help attract nonmembers; sponsor the annual pre–Mother's Day supper/program; and plan and direct the annual Men's Day program, which highlights the achievements of chosen individual brothers internally and externally to Trinity.

Men's Day Honorees

1971	Houston Stallworth, Man of the Year	Speakers: Mr. Aaron O. Cook, head of Macon Area Vocational Technical School Macon, Georgia
1972	Unknown	Reverend Sherman
1973	Vincent Murphy, Man of the Year	Deacon Hosea Waters
1974	Unknown	Reverend Alfred E. Barnes, assistant professor of social welfare, Fort Valley State College
1975	Robert Church, Man of the Year	Reverend E. S. Evans, Mount Olive Baptist Church, Macon, Georgia Theme: "To Serve the Present Age—My Call to Fulfill"
1976	Martin Edwards, Man of the Year Darold McCrary, Young Man of the Year	Reverend Curtis Hardnett
1977	Elijah Weatherspoon, Man of the Year Charles Langston, Jr., Young Man of the Year	Dr. Robert Threat, professor FVSC
1978	Unknown	Reverend Julius Simmons, pastor, Trinity Baptist Church, Fort Valley, Georgia
1979	Vincent Murphy, Man of the Year Phillip Jordan, Young Man of the Year	Reverend O. L. Blackshear, pastor Mt. Pleasant Baptist Church, Atlanta, Georgia
1980	Unknown	Reverend Calhoun Sims
1981	Unknown	Reverend Dr. Winfred Hope, pastor Ebenezer Baptist Church, Athens, Georgia Theme: "It's the Life That Counts"

1982	John Taylor, Man of the Year	Reverend Leon Styles Theme: "Young and Still Serving"
1983	Clifford Ponder, Man of the Year	Reverend H. L. McColumn, Sr., pastor Spring Hill Baptist Church Theme: "Brighten the Corner Where You Are"
1984	Philip Brewton, Man of the Year Victor Taylor, Young Man of the Year	Reverend Robert L. Holston, pastor Mazareth Baptist Church, Columbus, Georgia Theme: "Men Looking for Tomorrow Today"
1985	Unknown	Dr. David T. Shannon, Vice president academic dean, International Theological Seminary, Atlanta, Georgia Theme: "Men of Trinity, Keeping the Charge"
1986	Unknown	Mr. Levi Terrill, executive director, National Baptist Development Corporation, Atlanta, Georgia Theme: "In All Things Show Thyself A Patter of Good Work"
1987	Unknown	Attorney Gregory Homer, Fort Valley State College, Fort Valley, Georgia Theme: "Won to Christ—Win One"
1988	Unknown	Dr. Benjamin F. Lewis Theme: "Men of Trinity Reaching Out to Build the Kingdom"
1989	William D. Moorehead, Sr., Man of the Year	Attorney Michael L. Thurmond

1990	Robert Church, Man of the Year Gregory Street, Young Man of the Year	Dr. Oscar L. Prator, president, Fort Valley State College, Fort Valley, Georgia Theme: "Building Christian Manpower: Our Challenge for the Nineties"
1991	Unknown	Honorable W. Louis Sands, judge of Superior Courts of the Macon Judicial Court, Macon, Georgia Theme: "Trinity's Men—Good Neighbors in Action"
1992	Oliver Appling, Man of the Year	Reverend Ronald Toney, pastor Lizzie Chapel Baptist Church Macon, Georgia Theme: "Trinity: Thankful for God's Goodness through the Years"
1993	Robert Church, Community Man of the Year	Dr. Samuel D. Jolley, president, Morris Brown College, Atlanta, Georgia "Trinity's Men Making a Difference"
1994	Unknown	Mr. Douglas T. Porter, athletic director, Fort Valley State College, Fort Valley, Georgia Theme: "Trinity's Challenge: Developing Men and Youth for Christian Leadership"
1995	William D. Moorehead, Jr., Man of the Year John Demons, Community Man of the Year	Mr. James Deen. retired public school administrator, Alma, Georgia Theme: "Trinity's Men are Lights in a Dark Place"

1996	Sidney Hand, Man of the Year Claybon J. Edwards, Community Man of the Year Keary Weatherspoon, Young Man of the Year	Honorable Lynmore James, Georgia state representative, District 140 Theme: "In All Things Show Thyself a Pattern of Good Work" (Titus 2:7)
1997	Marquis Turner, Young Man of the Year	Reverend William B. Blount Theme: "Trinity's Men Leading the Way to Christ Before the Millennium"
1998	David Eaton, Man of the Year	Reverend George Smith, Trinity Baptist Church, Fort Valley, Georgia Theme: "Men of Trinity Taking Up the Cross"
1999	Amos Smith, Man of the Year Sabastian Walker, Young Man of the Year	Attorney Charles Jones Theme: "Trinity's Men: Empowering Young Men for Strong Christian Leadership in the New Millennium"
2000	Elijah Weatherspoon, Man of the Year Darius Turner, Young Man of the Year Alfred Ellis, Community Man of the Year	Honorable C. Jack Ellis, mayor, City of Macon, Macon, Georgia "Trinity 2000: Serving the Present Age"
2001	Isaiah Yarber, Man of the Year Justin Carter, Young Man of the Year Philip Brewton, Community Man of the Year Robert Church, Senior Male Award	Reverend Emory Lightfoot, Jr, pastor, Mt. Zion Circuit Church, Forsyth, Georgia Theme: "Men of Trinity Serving the Present Age"

2002	Gregory E. Moore, Man of the Year	Reverend J. S. Wright, pastor emeritus, Macedonia Baptist Church, Augusta, Georgia Theme: Men of Trinity Attempting Great Things for God"
2003	Richard Hogan, Man of the Year Douglas Miller, Young Man of the Year Donald H. Evans, Community Man of the year	Unknown
2004	Unknown	Reverend Dr. L. Perry McNeal, pastor, Jerusalem & Historic Mt. Pleasant Missionary Baptist Church
2005	Unknown	Unknown
2006	Unknown	Unknown
2007	Unknown	Unknown
2008	Unknown	Unknown
2009	Carson Caulwell, Man of the Year Saturn Aiken, Young Man of the Year Evangelist Al Sanders, Community Man of the Year	Reverend Dr. Efrem Yarber, associate minister Beulahland Baptist Church Theme: "Trinity Men Building the Kingdom through 'Inreach' and Outreach"
2010	James Morgan, Man of the Year Ronnie Moody, Jr., Young Man of the Year Clifford Ponder, Community Man of the Year	Reverend John Henry Neal, pastor, Greater St. Andrew Missionary Baptist Church, Climax, Georgia Theme: "Trinity Men Making Disciples by Loving God and Loving People" (Matthew 22:37–38)

2011	Unknown	Reverend Keith H. McIntosh, associate minister, New Hope Baptist Church, Perry, Georgia Theme: "Trinity Men Making Disciples by Casting Their Nets for Christ"
2012	Unknown	Attorney Gordon Lane "Jack" Joyner, esquire, Atlanta, Georgia
2013	Unknown	Theme: "Trinity Men Reaching Men by Meeting Men"
2014	Unknown	
2015	Albert O'Bryant, Man of the Year William Moore, Young Man of the Year John Demons, Community Man of the Year **Special Awards:** Philip Brewton Claybon Edwards	Reverend Terrell L. Brown, junior youth minister, Covenant Life Cathedral, Macon, Georgia Theme: "Trinity Men Building the Church on the Gospel of Christ"
2016	John Demons, Man of the Year Dontrell Harris, Young Man of the Year the Diplomats, Community Men of the Year	Dr. Bernard Hill, founder and senior pastor, Harvest Time Faith Center Church, Vidalia, Georgia Theme: "Trinity Men Doubling Discipleship"

Each year since 1971, the Ambassador Ministry has served as mentors for male youths through a number of activities in Fort Valley. In the 1960s, Boy Scout Troop 245, sponsored by Trinity, was organized. Henry E. Bryant, St Peters AME Church, was the Boy Scout commissioner for Peach County. David Cornelius served as scoutmaster with assistants David Eaton, William D. Morehead, and John Taylor. The support committee consisted of Wilma Anderson, Felma McCrary, Alma Simmons, Bessie Willis, Marvin Dyson, Jerry Martin, Vincent Murphy, and Elijah Weatherspoon.

Vincent Murphy, Sr., Vincent Murphy, Jr., and Isaac Crumbly served as chaperones to Atlanta Braves games (1967 and 1968). One of their successful fundraising activities was the selling of light bulbs.

The men assisted with a community baseball team organized by Willie (Bo) Davis, Central Union Baptist Church, in the early seventies. They provided support and guidance in teaching basic skills to the young boys. The men from Trinity were Vincent Murphy, Sr., David Eaton, David Cornelius, Elijah Weatherspoon, and Marvin Dyson.

In 2006, a fishing rodeo was initiated by David Eaton, who loved fishing as a hobby. He asked that the ambassadors teach the young boys ages twelve to fourteen how to fish. The first activity was held at the Georgia National Fairgrounds & Agricenter in Perry, Georgia. The boys were taught how to cast a fishing pole line, to be courteous not to get in the way of others fishing, how to bait the hook, how to safely remove the fish from the hook, and how to have fun. The boys enjoyed it so much that it became an annual affair. It was later named the David Eaton Fishing Rodeo in memory of the late Brother David Eaton, who passed away in 2008.

Pastor Gregory E. Moore emphasized that the church must focus its attention on discipling others. He expressed to the men that discipleship involves more than hearing, also depending on time spent with mentors, internalizing scripture, and developing a close relationship with Christ. If one expects great things from God, one must attempt to do great things for God. He initiated the first Men's Retreat, August 1–3, 2002, at Rock Eagle 4-H Center, located in the Oconee National Forest, Eastman, Georgia, its beauty and natural surroundings serving as an ideal place. The purpose of the retreat was to strengthen the Christian men in their spiritual growth for serving and making disciples. The men enjoyed it so much they planned a second retreat.

Among a list of activities is a special program called Men's Day. It is held annually on the third Sunday in September to recognize individuals for outstanding work and service to the church and the community. Awards are presented to recognize Man of the Year, Young Man of the Year (a teen), and Community Man of the Year. A fellowship breakfast is prepared for all ambassadors prior to the occasion on Saturday morning.

The ambassadors were recognized by The Mitchell Foundation, Inc., of Alabama for their work in the community of Fort Valley with a special donation of $1,000 in 1974. This was made possible through the efforts of Dr. and Mrs. Frank Vinson of

Fort Valley. Dr. Frank Vinson was a physician, and Mrs. Vinson was mayor from 1962–1964.

Other activities include but are not limited to a citywide cleanup day, Mother's Day tribute dinner, vacation Bible school picnic, obtaining reference books for pastor's office, outreach picnic, and Christmas 2003, with the Fort Valley Evening Optimist Club.

A quote from "Pastor's Pen" states the following: "The world needs Christian male leadership now more than ever before. As a church, we must do everything we can to teach men the responsibility God gave them to bear. They must perform their roles no matter what the consequences. He expects us to grow spiritually in disciplining ourselves to do God's will and to reach out and bring people to Christ."

The Sisterhood of Dorcas Ministry

The women of Trinity became an organized auxiliary under the leadership of Reverend E. F. Ridley, who saw a need to improve the appearance of the sanctuary. The Vigilante Club became an organized body in September 1952 with the election of three officers: Motta Simms (head of the Home Economics Department, FVSC), chairperson; Ruth Ross, cochairperson; and Mrs. Frank Hutchinson, secretary. The mission of this auxiliary was to improve the church edifice by making it a beautiful and an enjoyable place to worship. Its purpose was threefold: to beautify the church, to plan a special program in recognition of women, and to develop fundraising activities to supplement the church budget. Its meetings were planned for the first and third Sunday of each month.

The newly elected officers focused their attention on planning projects to beautify the interior and exterior of the church. The first project was to raise funds to purchase a carpet runner. In order to accumulate enough funds for the project, Daisy Lewis suggested that they open a special account, with each woman being responsible for donating three dollars. They continued with the purchase of dogwood trees for landscaping and improving the outside appearance of the church. Reverend William Smith (the present pastor) and the men were so pleased with the work done by the women that they added projects for them to sponsor.

Plans were also made to recognize the outstanding work of women in the church. Annie L. Clark was elected and given the honor of first "Woman of the Year," 1954. This title carried with it the special privilege of representing Trinity on special programs at other churches. The first Woman's Day program was initiated in 1958 as an annual affair during the presidency of Clita Jackson and honored the Woman of the Year. Julia Edwards was elected. The success of this program influenced the decision to make it not only an annual affair by honoring the Woman of the Year but also the Young Woman of the Year and at this time give recognition to the "Mother of the Church." Angeola Arnold was elected Woman of the Year, 1959, and Dorothy Hollinshed was the first "Young Woman of the Year, 1959. Annie Lou Gray, Lee Clara Allen, and Alberta Rumph have all served in succession as Mother of the Church.

Women's Day Honorees

1954	Annie L. Clark	Woman of the Year
1958	Julia Edwards	Woman of the Year
	Angeola Jackson Arnold	Honorable Mention
1959	Angeola Arnold	Woman of the Year
	Dorothy Hollinshed	Young Woman of the Year
1962	Mary Julia Marshall	Woman of the Year
1963	Alberta Moody	Woman of the Year
	Yvonne Beauford	Young Woman of the Year
1965	Annie M. Porter	Woman of the Year
	Jacqueline McCray	Young Woman of the Year
	Lorene Blue	College Woman of the Year
1968	Elizabeth J. Macomson	Woman of the Year
	Maude Price	College Woman of the Year
	Barbara Ann Arnold	Teen of the Year
	Lee Clara Allen	Mother of the Church
1969	Money Mae Talton	Woman of the Year
	Paulette McCray	Teen of the Year
	Mary Elizabeth Thompson	Young College Woman of the Year
	Lee Clara Allen	Mother of the Church
1970	Angeola Arnold	Woman of the Year
	Denise Cornelious	Young Woman of the Year
	Veronica Jackson	Young College Woman of the Year
	Lee Clara Allen	Mother of the Church
	Felma McCrary	Honorable Mention
	Evelyn McCray	Honorable Mention
	Doris Lavender	Honorable Mention
	Alberta Moody	Honorable Mention
	Mary Mathis	Honorable Mention
	Viola McGhee	Honorable Mention
	Loistine Smith	Honorable Mention

1971	Alberta Moody	Woman of the Year
	Patricia Simmons	Young Woman of the Year
	Jacqueline McCray	College Woman of the Year
	Lee Clara Allen	Mother of the Church
	Elizabeth Brinson	Honorable Mention
	Carrie Murphy	Honorable Mention
	Luetta McCrary	Honorable Mention
	Wilma J. Anderson	Honorable Mention
	Evangeline Williams	Honorable Mention
	Murlenun Hicks	Honorable Mention
	Mary Marshall	Honorable Mention
1972	Luetta McCrary	Woman of the Year
	Earnestine Green	College Woman of the Year
	Sharon Williams	Young Woman of the Year
	Lee Clara Allen	Mother of the Church
1973	Alma Simmons	Woman of the Year
1976	Willie D. Moorehead	Woman of the Year
	LaVoris McCrary	Young Woman of the Year
	Lee Clara Allen and Lillie B. Miller	Mothers of the Church
	Wilma Anderson	
	Mary Mathis	Honorable Mention
	Brenda Weatherspoon	Honorable Mention
		Honorable Mention
1977	Brenda Weatherspoon	Woman of the Year
	Cathy Williams	Young Woman of the Year
	Sharon Huggons	Teen of the Year
	Yvette Moorehead	Preteen of the Year
	Alice Mathis	Honorable Mention
	Mary Mathis	Honorable Mention
	Wilmetta Langston	Honorable Mention
	Alberta Rumph	Honorable Mention
	Money Mae Talton	Honorable Mention
	Corlis McCrary	Honorable Mention

	Jackie Smith	Honorable Mention
	Jamehl Demons	Honorable Mention
	Donna Bellamy	Honorable Mention
	Anita Lavender	Honorable Mention
1978	Doris Lavender	Woman of the Year
	Candace McCrary	Young Woman of the Year
	Millicent Singh	Young Woman of the Year
	Alberta Rumph	Mother of the Church
	Alice Davis	Honoree
	Ada Gadsden	Honoree
1979	Elizabeth Brinson	Woman of the Year
	Alberta Rumph	Mother of the Church
	Candace McCrary	Baptist Youth Fellowship
	Wilmetta Langston	Chancel Choir
	Lynette Moorehead	Children's Choir
	Celestine Johnson	Junior Usher Board
	Kimberly Mangrum	Katye Troup Usher Board
	Rilla King	Missionary
	Luetta McCrary	Senior Usher Board
	Robin Turner	Sunday School
	Sharon Huggins	Young People's Choir
1980	Alice Mathis	Woman of the Year
	Donnita Bellamy	Children's Choir
	Yvette Moorehead	Teenage Choir
	Cynthia Corker	Teenage Choir
	Lynnette Moorehead	Katye Troup Ushers
	Jacquelyn Demons	Chancel Choir
	Angeline Williams	Teenage Usher
	Money Mae Talton	Senior Usher
	Jacqueline Smith	Sunday School
	Donna Bellamy	Baptist Youth Fellowship
	Alberta Rumph	Missionary
	Evelyn D. McCray	Community Service

1981	Wilmetta Langston	Woman of the Year
	Anita Lavender	Young Woman of the Year
	Candace McCrary	Young Woman of the Year
	Alberta Rumph	Mother of the Church
1982	Evangeline Williams	Woman of the Year
	Cathy Williams	Young Woman of the Year
	Yvette Moorehead	Teenager of the Year
	Alberta Rumph	Mother of the Church
1983	Inez Brewton	Woman of the Year
	Phyllis Brewton	Young Woman of the Year
	Anne Thomas	Honoree
	Alberta Rumph	Mother of the Church
1984	Madie Cornelius	Woman of the Year
	Alberta Rumph	Mother of the Church
	Felma McCrary	Honorable Mention
	Louise Rouse	Honorable Mention
	Louise Sanders	Honorable Mention
	Daisy Canady	Honorable Mention
1986	Missionary Society Honored	
1987	Jacquelyn Demons	Woman of the Year
	Andrena Daniely	Young Woman of the Year
	Alberta Rumph	Mother of the Church
1988	Barbara Daniely	Woman of the Year
	Donnita Bellamy	Young Woman of the Year
	Alberta Rumph	Mother of the Church
1989	Elizabeth Hawkins	Woman of the Year
	Alberta Rumph	Mother of the Church
1990	Gloria Harris	Woman of the Year
	Andrena T. Daniely	College Woman of the Year
	Tomia Esperanza Palmer	Young Woman of the Year
	Alberta Rumph	Mother of the Church
1991	Hope Giles	Woman of the Year
	Katina Raquel Weatherspoon	Young Woman of the Year
	Alberta Rumph	Mother of the Church

1992	Faye Pugh Singh	Woman of the Year
	Melissa Faith Giles	Young Woman of the Year
	Alberta Rumph	Mother of the Church
	Missionary Society Honored	
1993	Bernice H. Eaton	Woman of the Year
	Alberta Rumph	Mother of the Church
1994	Ada Gadsden	Woman of the Year
	Alberta Rumph	Mother of the Church
1995	Dorothy N. Burns Conteh	Woman of the Year
	Alya Gabrielle Singh	Young Woman of the Year
	Mary Patterson Murray	Community Service Award
	Alberta Rumph	Mother of the Church
1996	Lillian Davis Kimbro	Woman of the Year
	Candice Nicole Magee	Young Woman of the Year
	Evelyn D. McCray	Community Service Award
	Alberta Rumph	Mother of the Church
1997	Money Mae Talton	Woman of the Year
	Tiffany Taylor	Young Woman of the Year
	Isabelle Freeman	Community Service Award
	Alberta Rumph	Mother of the Church
1998	Women of Trinity Honored	
	Alberta Rumph	Mother of the Church
1999	Thelma Juanita Hunter Bellamy	Woman of the Year
	Jenita Joann Barrett	Young Woman of the Year
	Faye Pugh Singh	Community Service Award
	Alberta Rumph	Mother of the Church
2000	Delia W. Taylor	Woman of the Year
	Wilmetta S. Langston	Community Service Award
2001	Hattie Floyd	Woman of the Year
	Dorothy Conteh	Community Service Award
2002	Jeanette K. Huff	Woman of the Year
	Annie Pearl Wilkerson	Community Service Award
2003	Mary Edwards	Woman of the Year
	Samantha Small	Young Miss

2004	Evelyn D. McCray	Woman of the Year
	Jessica Abrams	Young Woman of the Year
	Shavodus Plant	Teenager of the Year
	Jacquelyn Demons	Community Service Award
	Narissa Chamblis	Special Award
2005	Lorene Clemons McRae	Woman of the Year
	LaShauna J. Hunt	Young Woman of the Year
2006	Ruby H. Duffie	Woman of the Year
	Schenericka Abrams	Young Miss
2007	Karen Turner	Woman of the Year
	Helen Louise Moore	Young Woman of the Year
	Keia Turner	Young Miss
	Enola Dozier	Community Service Award
2008	J. Denise McCrary	Woman of the Year
	Bridget Colvard	Young Woman of the Year
	Shanequa L. Plant	Young Miss
	Constance Miller	Community Service Award
2009	Kathie Lockett	Woman of the Year
	Stephanie Burroughs Telfair	Young Woman of the Year
	Shnikea Talton	Young Teen of the Year
	Dr. Virginia Dixon	Community Service Award
2010	Elma J. Clayton Wells	Woman of the Year
	Samantha S. Small	Young Woman of the Year
	Ashley Latra Pepper	Young Miss
	Benita Donnette Scott	Young Miss
	Valaria Barden Mc Crary	Community Service Award
2011	Annie Pearl Z. Wilkerson	Woman of the Year
	Jakeisha M. Brown	Young Woman of the Year
	Courtney Denise Small	Young Miss
	Shonda Candis Fobbs	Community Service Award
2013	Donna Denise Bellamy	Woman of Outreach
	Vender Williams	Woman of Outreach
	Mary Yarber	Woman of Outreach
	Kristy Brewton Kenney	Community Service Award

2014	Dorothy Conteh	Woman of the Year
	Jessica Abrams	Young Woman of the Year
	Mary Grace Moore	Young Miss
	Shirley Schofield	Community Service Award
2015	Dr. Helen-Louise Moore	Woman of the Year
	Kasie Swayne	Young Woman of the Year
	The Honorable Patty James	Community Service Award
2016	All Women of Trinity	Honorable Mention

The Musical Candlelight Tea was a social activity event planned for community inter-action. Its first event was held on March 15, 1959, at the H. A. Hunt gymnasium, Spruce Street, Fort Valley, Georgia. It later became known as the "Candlelight Tea." Cultural and fine arts were exhibited. Some of these exhibitions included paintings by local artists from the Fort Valley Artist Club, Fort Valley, Georgia; African artifacts, Tubman Museum, Macon, Georgia; and collectible items from private collectors. Two noted black colleges appeared in concert. The Virginia Union College Glee Club, Richmond, Virginia, and the Spelman College Glee Club, Atlanta, Georgia, appeared in concert. Our own Jamehl Demons, daughter of John and Jacquelyn Demons, was a member of the Spelman Glee Club. Peach County High School, Macon County High School, and Fort Valley State College choirs participated on many occasions. Alice Mathis and Hattie Floyd two of our senior members recited poems by Paul Lawrence Dunbar from memory.

After a decade or more of existence, the name Vigilante Club became an issue. During the presidency of Mary Mathis, a discussion about changing the name of the club was recorded in the minute book dated January 12, 1969. It appeared that some of its members did not like the name "Vigilante." After some discussion, the issue was voted on, with eight "for a change" and four "against the change." The women, however, could not agree on a replacement name. Discussions sporadically appeared within the minutes over a four-year period, with several names submitted as possibili-ties: Trinettes, Vigilantes, Dorcas Club, TWAC (Trinity Women Ambassadors Club), Peacemaker's Club, and Bykota Club. The members were unsuccessful in getting a majority vote. It was not until 1973 that Daisy Lewis suggested that the names be given to Reverend Simmons to make the decision. Reverend Simmons chose two names: Bereaons, taken from Acts 17:10, and Circle of Dorcas, taken from Acts 9:36–43. "Dorcas," he explained, "also called Tabitha, gave much of her time to making gar-ments for the poor. She caused many to accept Christianity." Carrie Murphy, president in 1973, addressed the group and presented the names given by Reverend Simmons. The name "Dorcas" was approved on April 15, 1973. The organization became known as Dorcas, and today is referred to as Sisterhood of Dorcas Ministry.

Fundraising Events

The Vigilante Club, later known as Dorcas, spearheaded many fundraising events to supplement the church budget. Traditionally, black churches, being the first community or public institutions that the blacks actually owned and completely controlled, were supported from dues and fundraising activities. Trinity's dues were one dollar per month for adults, twenty cents for children. Its church service was held twice a month, on the first and third Sunday. Ward leaders in the church were responsible for collecting the dues. The first Sunday's collection went to the pastor, and the third Sunday's collection was for the church. Most of the money that helped toward financing the church was raised from box suppers and fish fries. Sandwiches were prepared by the women and sold for ten cents at church rallies. The choir helped raise money by giving performances at other churches. Mock weddings were also excellent fundraising events.

Whether under the supervision of Dorcas or presented as an all-church activity, the fundraising activities continued throughout its history. The events varied and had many titles, such as rallies for thanksgiving, the united nations, anniversary, building fund, birthdays, the continents and the seasons, and so forth. Angeola Arnold introduced the birthday rally. This idea originated with the Gano PTA during the early fifties and was used for more than a decade as their annual fundraising project. This all-church birthday celebration became a popular event. It was governed by guidelines featuring two specific categories. The first category was table design; a unique floral arrangement representing each month. The twelve table arrangements would be judged, with first-, second-, and third-place winners, according to theme, creativity, and appearance. The second category was competition. Each month competed to raise the most money. The outcome of the second annual birthday party was announced in the *Leader Tribune*, July 24, 1975. The first-place winner for table arrangement went to the month of September (Angeola Arnold, chairperson); the month of July won second place (Evangeline Williams, chairperson); the month of May won third place, (Ernest Corker, chairperson). The fundraising winners included first place, September (Angeola Arnold, chairperson); second place, July (Evelyn McCray, chairperson); third place, May (Ernest Corker, chairperson). The committee members were Angeola Arnold, Hattie Banks, Alice Mathis, Evangeline

Williams, and Ernest Corker. The judges were Gladys Grace, Rosa Lee Gilbert, and Ruth Allen. Annie Mae Porter, known for her beautiful flower arrangements, was recognized for her creativity for the award-winning September table display.

The competition increased at the third annual all-church birthday party, held on September 30, 1976. The first place winner was the month of April, who chose the theme "April Showers" (Gladys Sampson, chairperson); the second place winner was January, with the theme "Should Auld Acquaintance Be Forgot" (Evangeline Williams, chairperson); the third place winner was July, with our country's "Our Bicentennial Birthday" as its theme (Alberta Moody, chairperson). The first-place winner for having raised the most money went to the month of August, with $1,020 (Annie P. Wilkerson, chairperson); the second-place winner was the month of July, with $649 (Alberta Moody, chairperson); the third place winner was the month of September, with $490 (Robert Church, chairperson).

Another celebration was the 1976 bicentennial event celebrating our country's two hundredth anniversary. This bicentennial celebration (1976) was ongoing throughout the year. The planning committee members were Angeola Arnold, Evangeline Williams, Alice Mathis, Jacqueline Demons, Robert Church, and Bernice Eaton. An invitation was sent to friends and family, requesting their attendance at the Sunday morning worship service on April 11, 1976. The congregation was encouraged to participate by wearing outfits depicting clothing worn by our ancestors. The congregation sang hymns and spiritual songs (a cappella style). The costumes were judged, with winners selected for best costume: William E. Arnold was crowned Mr. Bicentennial, and Alberta Rumph (Johnson) was crowned Mrs. Bicentennial. The youths were judged and crowned as Junior Mr. Bicentennial (Theodore Talton) and Junior Miss Bicentennial (LaVoris McCrary). The congregation fellowshipped together, enjoying the prepared box dinners served on the church lawn.

The most popular events were the children's contests. The parents, relatives, and sponsors went all out to make them winners. A "Little Miss Bicentennial" and "Miss Preteen Bicentennial" pageant was presented on August 28, 1976. The contestants for Little Miss Bicentennial were Katina Weatherspoon, Andrea Strickland, and Erica Smith. Katina Raquel Weatherspoon was crowned Little Miss Bicentennial. Her brother Kevin Genard Weatherspoon was her escort. Seven young girls vied for "Miss Preteen Bicentennial." They were Andrena Daniely, Tanja Davis, Millicent Singh, Anita Lavender, Candance McCrary, Jamehl LaRue Demons, and Muriel Harris. Andrena Daniely was crowned "Miss Preteen Bicentennial." Rodney Horton was her escort.

The "Little Miss Fort Valley" event was held June 11, 1978, with contestants Tatania

Fluellen, Mia Fabra Mathis, Celeste Ponder, and Juandolyn Turner escorted by Jamal Starlling, José Dixon, Dexter Street, and Jeffrey Turner. "The Prince and Princess in the Magic Kingdom," sponsored by Dorcas, was presented April 28, 1984. The nursery rhyme characters were Patrice L. Daniels, Little Bo Peep; Casey Felton, Old King Cole; Alya Singh, Little Miss Muffet; Gregory Bernard Street, Little Boy Blue; Ramonia Mathis, Little Polly Flinders; Taneka Dixon, Queen of Hearts; Victor Vance, Hey, Diddle, Diddle; Ricky Hogan, Little Jack Horner; and Paron J. Simmons, Pat-a-Cake. The program committee members were Inez Brewton, Barbara Daniely, Marie Cleveland, Doris Lavendar, Faye Singh, and Gloria Street. The winner for the "The Little Miss Princess" contest was Katina Weatherspoon. The "Little Miss Sweetheart" was a special contest sponsored by the Dorcas Club on February 13, 1983, in an effort to raise funds to rebuild our storm-damaged sanctuary. Inez Brewton, chairperson, and her committee raised $9,400.

Publicity in the local papers was important to keep the public informed of the ongoing activities at the community churches. Katye Troup wrote a social column called "Dits, Dashes & Dots of Fort Valley, Georgia" for the *Pittsburgh Courier*, a weekly newspaper that circulated nationwide in most of the black communities. The articles were informative in keeping the public knowledgeable concerning events in Fort Valley and the surrounding areas.

One of Troup's many articles consisted of an informal meeting (circa 1957) at the comfortable, cozy home of Doris Lavendar, where plans were made for a Vigilante activity. Present for this occasion were Murlenum Hicks, Inez Smith, Willie D. Moorehead, R. N. Thompson, Loistene Smith, K. C. Troup, Delia Towns, Wilma J. Anderson, and Daisy Lewis. Another (circa 1954) reported plans being made for Trinity's Women's Day and Rally Day celebration at the home of Mrs. Benjamin S. Anderson. Present for this meeting were Inez Smith, Vivian Anderson, M. Hicks and K. C. Troup.

Other reporters were Wilma Anderson from Trinity Baptist Church and Evelyn W. Robinson, Usher Temple's CME, who wrote a column called "Around Our Town" for the *Leader Tribune*, a local newspaper. Many of the local programs were shared in their column.

The Sisterhood of Dorcas's contributions have been many throughout the years—from decorations in the sanctuary, items for the kitchen, a money tree for the pastor, or special dinners for the congregation. The organization has been self-sufficient, with funds contributed by an assessment of dues and through fundraising events. It has also been generous in its contribution to the church budget. In 1980, the amount of $800 was given to the financial treasurer for the upkeep of the church.

It was under the leadership of Ruby Duffie, president 1999–2000, that two new programs, "Guess Who's Coming to Dinner" and "The First Lady Day" were implemented. The first was a fun-filled activity of dining and fellowship at the homes of volunteer hosts. The women were divided into groups, and each group appeared at a different home to dine. The second event was to give tribute to First Lady Alma A. Simmons for the work she did in supporting her husband in his ministry as well as her service and spiritual commitment to God. First Lady Simmons was a college librarian serving in the area of teacher education at Fort Valley State University. She served on the usher board, as a deaconess and on the Missionary Ministry. She sang with the special Women's Day Choir and was visible and supportive in all activities and programs at Trinity. She was very busy with two active children, Patricia Diane and Julius C. (Jay) Simmons, Jr., and grandchildren, Julius III (Paron), Ravin, and Christian Young. Paron grew up in Trinity.

This event continued with a tribute to First Lady Dr. Helen Louise Moore. An appreciation tea was given August 16, 2014, at the Courtyard Marriot's Falcon Room, Warner Robins, Georgia. This affair was for women only, with the theme "Hats off to Our First Lady." Dr. Moore also devoted much of her time and talent supporting her husband's ministry as pastor of Trinity while working as a full-time pediatrician and mother of three children, William, Mary Grace, and Christiana. With her busy schedule around the clock and taking care of children, she knew who was the head of her life and who gave her strength to serve as a leader, speaker, teacher, advisor, and a role model to youth and young adults as well as others who came in contact with her at church, in the community, or at the office.

The Pastor's support ministry spearheaded a combined fifteenth pastors anniversary and First Lady, gala. Talisha Moody chaired this activity. This semiformal affair was held August 2016 at the Austin Theatre, Fort Valley, Georgia. Special guests included relatives, friends of the family, and guest ministers. In ministers in attendance were Reverend Dr. and Mrs. K. D. Dawsey, Reverend and Mrs. David Stanley, Reverend and Mrs. Efrem Yarber.

The Music Ministry

The role of the choir has always been to provide musical selections for the church. Music and worship go hand in hand. Music gives a spiritual uplift in preparing the audience to hear God's Word. Music has always been a part of our black culture—from the old spiritual hymns to the contemporary gospels. Since 1912, Lelia Felder (founder) and daughter Leslie Davis shared a vision that music could be used at Trinity to unite people in service to the Lord. The congregation sang in a cappella style, touching hearts as they lifted up their voices in complete harmony in praise to the Lord. Emma Walker, Connie

Miller, and Gussie Chellers also loved music. They visualized the role music could play in the church service by organizing a choir. Included were a number of piano players who also rendered service to the church: Connie Miller, Emma Walker, Mary Miller, Lessie Davis, Lelia Felder, Thelma Baldwin, Gussie Chellers, Rena Jackson, Ethel Jackson Stamps, Rosa Isom, and Gertis Williams Simmons. Some of the early choir members (1929) were Celeles (Chellers), Tommie Daniel, Annie Lee Emanual, Rosa Lee Emanuel, Johnnie C. Davis, Nellie Young (Jackson), Louise Young (Sanders), Rosa Young (Richards), Arthur C. Young, Jr., Martha Morgan (Simmons), Angeola Jackson (Arnold), Lewis Johnson, Odell Robinson Johnson, and Hattie Humphrey Floyd.

Emma Walker organized a youth choir called the Sunbeams. They sang at Sunday school, state conventions, and Baptist Training Union (BTU) programs. Katye Troup, First Lady, Fort Valley State College, assisted, and together they conducted voice training for the youth. She was an influential role model to the youths and the adults. Everything had to be correct and in order, and she did not hesitate to let you know.

Mary Edwards Marshall and Evelyn Davis McCray expressed some of their experiences in the youth choir. They both sang soprano. They were encouraged to "hit the high notes." Marshall remembered how she enjoyed imitating Sister Emma and practiced to make sure her voice pitch would reach the high notes. The Edwards residence was on Pine Street, directly behind the church sanctuary. While she was doing her Saturday chores, she explained, she could hear the adult choir practicing for Sunday worship service. This encouraged her to sing along with the choir while trying to get the high notes as instructed. During Evelyn's recollections, she said she especially liked the special treat at the El Morocco Grill, located on Carver Drive, that came after practice. It was a nice place to eat and listen to music on the jukebox. Unlike today, children were not allowed without parental guidance. McCray stated, "being chaperoned by Walker was the only way their parents would let them go." The Sunbeams Choir later became known as the Trinity Baptist Youth Choir.

Edward Moore came to Fort Valley in 1947 as an instructor of music at Fort Valley State College. He was a native of Columbus, Ohio, where he completed his degree in music and did further study at the Juilliard School of Music in New York City. He became associated with Trinity as pianist and director of the adult choir. During his tenure, 1947 to 1964, the choir rented an organ to add to the melody tendered by the piano. Dr. C. V. Troup served as organist. Moore taught piano lessons to children in the community. The Vigilante Club honored him in 1964 with a recital composed by his community students to show appreciation for his seventeen years of service to Trinity and to Fort Valley.

Murlenum Hicks and her family arrived the same year as Edward Moore. Hicks taught in the public school system of Peach County. Her husband, Dr. Odess Hicks, taught French and was head of the Foreign Languages Department at Fort Valley State College. The Hickses and their two daughters, Marian and Carolyn, became active members of Trinity. Hicks's avocation was music, and she and her husband immediately became members of the choir. With the resignation of Moore, Murlenum Hicks filled the vacancy and served as pianist and choir director. She later became organist when the Troup family moved to Atlanta in 1966.

A young couple by way of Columbus and Cairo, Georgia, met while students at Fort Valley State College. They joined in holy matrimony in 1974 and made Trinity their home church in Fort Valley. Brenda Weatherspoon taught music in the public school system, and Elijah Weatherspoon coached football. They became active members of the choir and often sang lead solos. Brenda became known for her talent and creativity, and it did not take long for her to team up with Sister Hicks, along with Dr. Bessie Willis, professor of music at the college and Trinity's musician. Together they began plans for a choir anniversary and a special Christmas program.

The choir anniversary was presented on November 3, 1974, with Elijah Weatherspoon as presider. The combined adult, youth, and children's choir participated. W.D. Moorehead directed the children's choir. Special guest churches were invited to render two selections. The guest churches in attendance were Belvin AME, Bethesda Baptist, Central Union Baptist, Cool Spring Baptist, Davis Hill Baptist, First Born Holiness, Fort Valley State Gospel Choir, Friendship Baptist, Free Run Baptist, Gilliard AME, Gordan Chapel AME, Gospel Movement Church, Holy Five, Greater Union Baptist, Mount Pleasant Baptist, Richland Baptist, St Louis CME, St Luke's Episcopal, St Peters AME, Shiloh Baptist, Spirits of Joy, and Usher's Temple CME. Ida Maddox, a former choir member (1929), recited a poem, and Wilma Anderson presented a special recognition to Murlenun Hicks, Evelyn Beauford, Mary Julia Marshall, Doris Lavender, Evelyn McCray, and Martha Simmons for their years of continuous service as choir members.

Brenda directed her first "Carol of Christmas" choir performance December 15, 1974. Evelyn Beauford served as the narrator. This program was dedicated to Dr. and Mrs. O. E. Hicks, Ms. Wilma Anderson, and Reverend and Mrs. J.C. Simmons. By this time, the choir had grown and become more organized. Evelyn Beauford served as president, Ada Gadsden as secretary-treasurer. The following year, 1975, Weatherspoon was elected choir director. She, along with Reverend Simmons, was instrumental in changing the name of the adult choir to the Chancel Choir. Serving as choir directors, Weatherspoon and Hicks invited James Harris, a well-known and talented FVSC music student from Macon County, to accompany them in presenting an arrangement of classical Christmas music by the Chancel Choir. Trinity's first Christmas cantata, "The Birth of Christ," was presented in December of 1975. "A Song Unending," by John W. Peterson, was directed by Weatherspoon and presented December 11, 1977. W. D. Moorehead accompanied on the piano and organ. The narrator on program was Mayor pro tem Claybon J. Edwards. Faye Lewis Strong, Columbus, Georgia, was special guest soloist. Other guest soloists were Phil Ballard, tenor, and Reginald Garrard, baritone. The cantata received rave reviews from the community. Comments also appeared in the church bulletin, including the following: "The Chancel Choir presented an excellent Christmas cantata … The setting was breathtaking, the music was heavenly, and the fellowship was super. We shall be eternally thankful to Mrs. Brenda Weatherspoon, Mrs. O. E. Hicks, and Mr. James Harris." The instant success of the Christmas cantata made it an annual affair, with a chain of performances directed by Sister Weatherspoon from 1977 to 2008. In 1978, she presented John W. Peterson's "Love Transcending." Dr. W. W. E. Blanchet, FVSC president, 1966–1973, was the narrator.

In 1980, Brenda S. Weatherspoon was elected to serve as the first minister of music to manage all of the church's music and musicians. She continued as director of the Chancel Choir and pianist.

During the eighties, she invited individuals from other churches to participate with the choir as guest performers: Joseph Adkins, Alfred Ellis, Jr., Edward McGee, Elizabeth White, Betty S. Willingham, Wyonnie Hardee, Reginald Garrard, James Harris, Faye Lewis, Randolph Lindsey, Joselyn Miller, Doris Rice, Birdelle Jackson, James Jackson, Clarence Moore, Jimmy L. Williams, Woody Freeman, Clara Martin, Vernon Harleston, Ulysses T. Sampson, and Robert Williams, to name a few. William S. Mathis and William Moultrie, accompanists, were on the piano and organ. The choir adhered to an agenda of serious practices beginning several months ahead, in September, to prepare for the upcoming annual event. A performance titled "Joy to the World," by John W. Peterson, was presented December 14, 1980. In formal attire, the concert choir made their grand entrance as they marched in procession into the sanctuary to take their designated places. The director stepped forward to the director's platform as the audience waited in awe for the raising of the wand and the first musical note to begin. The programs were beautifully designed and arranged to represent Christmas. The director's contacts brought not only guest soloists to sing but also instrumental musicians and narrators to set the tone and convey the story. Attorney Gregory Homer served as narrator.

The community audience grew each year, along with the number of individuals who participated in the musical. The cantata titled "A Song Unending," by John W. Peterson was repeated on December 12, 1982. Due to the renovation of Trinity's storm-damaged sanctuary, the place for this event had to be rescheduled. Usher's Temple CME Church graciously gave permission to use their church. Dollie Horton was narrator. Accompanying at the piano and organ were James Harris and Greg Stripling. Another accomplishment for Brenda was a performance with two churches some distance apart. Under the direction of Brenda Weatherspoon and Faye Lewis Strong, the M. L. Harris United Methodist Church's Chancel Choir, Columbus, Georgia, was invited to unite in concert with Trinity. Three consecutive cantatas were presented during a span of three years: "A Son! A Savior!" December 11, 1988; "Make His Praise Glorious," December 10, 1989; and "A Christmas Celebration," December 9, 1990.

Weatherspoon challenged the choir in making each performance the best it could be. She directed a long list of Christmas cantatas.

She presented an all-male Christmas choir with an arrangement of "Men Sing Christmas," 2000. The narrators were Reverend Gregory Homer, Sr.; Gregory Homer, Jr.; and Philip Brewton. Jeanette K. Huff, a member of the choir, wrote the script. The participants were Anthony Boynton, Philip Brewton, Alton Carson, Cullen Carson, Foster Carson, Lawrence Clarington, Arnold Giles, Fred Hill, James Jackson, Terry Johnson, Brian Jones, Randolph Lindsey, William Moultrie, Donnie Nicholson, Gus Oglesby, Corey Palmer, Thomas J. Palmer, Darnell Robinson, Allen Stripling, John Taylor, Jr., Clyde L. Turner, Elijah Weatherspoon, and Curtis West. Members of the Fort Valley State University male Glee Club participated.

In 2005, a younger generation stepped forward to assist. "His Plan" was directed by Jessica Abrams, Donna Bellamy, Faye Strong Boyer, and Brenda Weatherspoon. The participants included the combined choirs, the newly organized Julius C. Simmons Gospel Choir, and the Praise team and Mime dancers. The Mime dancers were directed by Christopher Croom.

The anniversary and Christmas events were only two of the many programs presented by the Chancel Choir. The choir kept a very busy schedule of events, from the worship service to revivals to special event performances. Some of these events included performances at the Warner Robins Civic Center, January 25, 1976. An event on August 8, 1976, featured the Weatherspoon Family, the Hillsman Sisters, and the Angelic Trio. A "Sing into Spring" concert was presented on June 5, 1977. The McCray family presented a musical tribute to Trinity called "Our Spiritual Roots" on

July 31, 1977. The Chancel Choir, in their commitment toward community outreach, conducted performances with the Peach Festival Choir, the Fort Valley Community Choir, the FVSC Distinguished Service Award program, the FVSC president inaugural luncheon, and FVSC commencement exercises. The Women's Day choir and Men's Day choir were special presentations for the occasion.

Other musicians were Willie D. Moorehead, who served as director for the youth choir and children's choir for a number of years. As director in 1975, she presented Christmas music to an audience of downtown listeners in Fort Valley. Under her direction, the youth sang during a closing session of the Union Missionary Baptist Association in 1975. She came to Fort Valley in the late 1950s with her husband, William D. Moorehead, Sr. She taught music in the Peach County school system and private music lessons in her home to community children. She also conducted and began a children's program for younger children. She was church organist when Jacqueline Prater vacated the position. She opened and closed the worship service with a rendition of beautiful chimes. Moorehead served on the Sisterhood of Dorcas Ministry as well as being accompanist for the many programs presented at Trinity. The Mooreheads and their children, Wynette, Yvette, Lynette, and Douglas, were very visible at Trinity. Yvette, having been taught piano lessons by her mother, was interested in learning to play the church organ. She later became organist for Trinity while a student at Peach County High School.

Jacqueline Polson Prater, First Lady, Fort Valley State College, joined Trinity with her husband, Dr. Oscar Prater, president, Fort Valley State College. She served as organist until her health failed in 1998. Audrey Magee served as pianist and organist. Cheryl Dickerson served as musician and director of the children's choir, composing most of the music and songs for the children. She was also active with vacation Bible school.

Faye Strong Boyer sang as guest soloist in many of the Christmas cantatas. She later moved to Fort Valley from Columbus, Georgia, and joined Trinity's Chancel Choir. She was appointed director of music. Others who served were David Henry, Gregory Miller, Renee Sneed, Garfield Fobbs (2010–2013), and AlDevin Jackson (2013–2016). Joseph Thomas was appointed minister of music in 2017. Other musicians were Joe Thomas, assistant choir director; David Kerr, saxophonist; Calandra Jones, guitarist; Keith Wilson, bass guitarist, Kerry Weatherspoon, drummer, and Leonard Giles, bass guitarist.

The Julius C. Simmons Gospel Choir was organized in 2002. Tamia Palmer accepted the position to serve as director. She grew up in Trinity and returned to Fort Valley to begin practicing medicine after completing her medical degree. Jeanette Huff served as administrative assistant. Gregory Black was recruited as pianist/organist. Brother Greg, as he was sometimes called, loved to play the piano and organ as well as sing gospel songs. Jessica Abrams followed Palmer as director. The choir members were Jessica Abrams, Linda Abrams, Jenita Barrett, Donnita Bellamy, Philip Brewton, Grace Corker, Dorothy Crumbly, Barbara Daniely, Cheryl Dickerson, Mary Edwards, Willie Foster, Hope Giles, Gloria Harris, Anita Hogan, T. J. Hogan, Jeanette Huff, Mary Julia Marshall, Addie Nelson, Barbara Palmer, Corey Palmer, Thomas Palmer, Faye Singh, Mattie Turner, Brenda Weatherspoon, Elijah Weatherspoon, and Geneva West.

The Youth Ministry

The children and young adults were actively involved throughout the history of Trinity. Their directors, sponsors, and/or chairpersons in charge sought to raise their quality of life by beginning a number of programs designed especially for teaching youth to develop good Christian principles and leadership skills. They attended Sunday school, vacation Bible school, and children's church. Some were active participants in the children's choir, teenage choir, or youth choir.

Special programs were presented during anniversaries and for Mother's Day. "A Youth in Action for Christ: We Have Come a Long Way" was presented November 8, 1972, during an anniversary celebration. Presiding at this event was: Corlis McCrary and Wynette Moorehead. The program participants were Gregory Corker, Phillip Jordon, Patricia Simmons, Anita Lavender, Cynthia Corker, Vendya Cornelious, and Karen Marshall, along with Dwalla and Eric Simmons from St Peter AME Church. "A Tribute to Mothers" was another special program, featuring Lee Clara Allen as Mother of the Church, May 11, 1975. The program participants were Denise McCrary, Sharon Huggins, Jeffrey Jordan, Phillip Jordan, Darold McCrary, Corlis McCrary, Gregory Corker, Jamehl Demons, Felice Dyson, Anita Ponder, LaVoris McCrary, Chauncil Talton, Karen Talton, Kathy Talton, Julius (Jay) Simmons, Alex McCrary, Anita McCray, Ronnie Moody, Tangie Dyson, Jackie Smith, Felicia Jordon, David Eaton, Alan Brantley Richie, Arita Edwards, Denise Edwards, and Angelina Williams.

Youth in Sunday School

Preparing children to learn was important to the leaders working with children in the church. Very early on, the children were taught not only to read the scripture but also to pray when called to do so and to participate in programs. The young adult was elected or chosen to serve as Sunday school secretary. She or he was taught to record the minutes each Sunday. The first Sunday school minute book located among Trinity's church records was a handwritten composition book dated 1938–1939. Eloise Edwards, secretary, recorded names of classes and teachers, the number in attendance, and offerings. Another minute book (1961–1971) was more advanced. It was designed for record keeping, with fill-in blanks for each Sunday session. Yvonne Beauford, 1961–1966, and Jacqueline McCray, 1967–1971, were recorders during this period. The records also listed individuals who served in various acting positions working as secretary, conducting prayer, reading the scripture, or giving individual class reports. Some of the names in attendance appearing on record were Katherine Durham, Barbara Arnold, Denise Cornelius, Gail McCray, Veronica Jackson, Sharon Williams, and Diane Edwards, with Lewis Roberts serving as acting secretary. Others included Vincent Murphy, Jr., Larry Daniely, Melvin Murphy, Larry Latimore, Llewellyn Murphy, Barbara Martin, Jacquelyn McCray, Agnes White, Paulette McCray, Katherine Durham, Cynthia Beauford, Cassandra Edwards, Gloria Hollinshed, Gordan Joyner, Diane Edwards, Eloise Joyner, Harriette Beauford, Leon Hollinshed, Yvonne Mapp, Gail McCray, Louis Roberts, Naomi Lee, Denise Cornelius, Marilyn Mitchell, Patricia Simmons, Maude Price, Johnny Early, Rose Marie Mosley, Sherry Lowman, Johnny Davis, Paul Tompkins, Donald Williams, Mary Daniels, Mary Booker, Patricia Clark, Veronica Jackson, Vernon Campbell, Ricky Mathis, Brenda Camp, Connie Jackson, Beulah King, Irene Blue, Margaret Lee, Myrtle Wooden, Alfred Edwards, Andrew Edwards, Catherine Moore, M. Wooden, Frederick Cornelius, Beverly Turner, Vivian Williams, Wanda Jackson, Samuel Beauford, Avis McCray, Robert Price, Phillip Lavender, and Raynelle Moore. The superintendent also trained some of the young adult males to serve in this role.

Vacation Bible School

Vacation Bible school was a vital part of the Sunday school. Its beginning date is unknown. A vacation Bible school picture in the collection, dated 1951, shows Reverend Joseph E. Tackett, pastor, with community children and teachers. Osie Daniely Lindsey identified some of these. The teachers were Sisters Hodge, Murlenum Hicks, [Mary Hayes?], and Marnesha Tackett.

According to Barbara Daniely, vacation Bible school coordinator, vacation

Bible school serves as another avenue for bringing children and adults together in teaching and learning about the Bible. The volunteer teachers create many oppor-tunities for children to have fun while learning about God. It may be the beginning of learning "who Christ is" for some, while for others, it may be a renewal in studying His Word. Its sessions can help children in developing social skills through friendship with one another and assist-ing in the beginning of family Bible discussions at home. It provides a variety of educational ac-tivities outside of the classroom that can be ben-eficial in one's life. Participants are assigned to classes according to age level—beginners, pri-mary, juniors, seniors, and adults. The weeklong activity during the first part of the summer is scheduled after public school closing. The chil-dren and parents look forward to these fun- filled activities.

Vacation Bible School

Youth Choirs

The youth choir did not show a continuous pattern as the adult choir did. Willie D. Moorehead, Annie Weldon, Brenda Weatherspoon, Audrey McGhee, Cheryl Dickerson, Pricilla Bingham, and Katina W. T. Kendrick served as directors.

A youth choir activity program at Trinity, dated March 8, 1959 appeared in an issue of the *Pittsburgh Courier* newspaper. Miss Dorothy Hollinshed served as president of the youth choir, and James Isom was choir director. Reverend Julius C. Simmons was the speaker. The participants were Ruby Reese, Helen Thornton, Marva Hackney, Vascille Faulk, Dorothy Hollinshed, Jewell Hollinshed, Yvonne Wright, Julius Mason, John McNeil, William Coleman, F. Maxwell, James Isom, Louis Smith, Alfred Smith, Daniel Hopkins, Howard Lee, and Mr. and Mrs. George Jennings.

The Baptist Youth Fellowship

The Baptist Youth Fellowship came into being February 1978, after Inez Brewton approached Reverend Julius C. Simmons, requesting permission to form a Christian education program for our children. Reverend Simmons gladly granted her request and asked that an advisor council be formed. The first advisory council members were Inez Brewton, Barbara Daniely, Jacquelyn Demons, Ada Gadsden, Lillian Kimbro, Wilmetta Langston, Evelyn McCray, Faye Singh, Gloria Street, Delia Taylor, Brenda Weatherspoon, and Kathy Williams. The duties of the sponsors were to work with the Baptist Youth Fellowship for three age groups: Group I, ages five through eleven; Group II, ages twelve through eighteen; and Group III, collegiate. The BYF mission was encouraging youth to give their lives to the Lord. The objectives were that each student acquired the basic survival skills of life prior to high school graduation.

1. To be able to introduce a speaker
2. To become a speaker
3. To know proper dress attire for church and business
4. To be able to preside at a meeting using basic parliamentary procedure
5. To practice giving tithes and offering
6. To commit to daily scripture reading
7. To attend and participate in programs
8. To preside over a program

The advisors developed workshops for the youths to attend. Brenda Weatherspoon conducted the music workshops. Mary Huggins was the administrator for the Health and Abstinence workshops. Ada Gadsden, Wilmetta Langston, and Gloria Harris provided lessons for preteens during the worship service. Ada Gadsden was sponsor for the youth choir. Inez Brewton and Annie P. Wilkerson were advisors for the Katye Troup Ushers.

The first BYF Youth Day program was dated January 7, 1979. "Courage" was the theme. The program participants were Anita Ponder, president; Anita Lavender, secretary; John Taylor, III, treasurer; Cedric Ford, vice president; Phyllis Brewton, vice president. The following groups were included: Group I, Kirk Huggins, vice president; Group II, Robin Turner, assistant secretary; Charles Langston, III, reporter; Sharon Huggins, historian; and Angeline Williams, parliamentarian and sergeant at arms. The BYF had community service projects such as Group I: annual Thanksgiving basket, and Group II: annual Christmas cards to prison inmates. John Taylor III designed a BYF stamp for use on the cards, programs, and so on.

The youth choir and ushers participated during the annual revival. It became known as "Youth Rally." The Youth Rally "Living for Jesus" program, dated April 6, 1979, presented Reverend Donald Sneed, Greater Union Baptist Church, as speaker.

A Youth Rally play, *Shaping a Better Tomorrow*, was written by Angeline Williams for the revival and presented March 28, 1980. The characters were Ronnie Moody, Beverly Hand, Jamehl Demons, Charles Langston, Millicent Singh, Felicia Jordan, Yvette Moorehead, Kirk Huggins, Kelvin Morgan, Averil McCrary, and Cheryl Marshall (St. Luke Episcopal Church). Other participants in the program were Donnita Bellamy, Anita Lavender, Candace McCrary, and Donna Bellamy. Recognition was given to the talented individuals who designed the artwork and music: John Taylor, Jr., program cover design; Donna Bellamy, Brenda Weatherspoon, and John Taylor, Jr., scrapbook; Kathy Williams and Philip Brewton, art; W. D. Moorehead and Annie K. Weldon, music.

Trinity's youth were encouraged to be active participants in Sunday school and the Baptist Youth Fellowship. In addition, many served on other church auxiliaries: children's choir, Katye Troup Ushers, teenage choir, and teenage ushers. The BYF members recorded from programs and not listed above are Celestine Johnson, Alfred Conteh, Alvin Conteh, Lesli Burton, Lori Michelle Burton, Genard Weatherspoon, Alya Singh, Cynara Nelson, Felice Palmer, Tomia Palmer, Katina Weatherspoon, Daphne Walker, Celeste Ponder, Michelle McRae, Perry Mangrum, Keisha Ponder, Roni Mathis, Dexter Street, Derrick Meadows, Deirdre McGhee, Ernest McRae, Jr., Casey Felton-Arnold, Paron J. Simmons, Candice Magee, Niki Ross, Floyd Thomas, Bradley Carthon, Darian Magee, Melissa Giles, Teri Givens, Walter Mathis, Yvette Moorehead, Philip Jordan, and Candace McCrary. During the regular worship hour, the BYF presented Sunday school attendance awards and recognized Trinity's graduates. The graduate having the highest GPA gave the address. Deidre Eaton gave the address in 1981.

The BYF didn't only encourage youths to give their lives to the Lord. The curricula provided a long list of developmental skills that introduced them to biblical history: learning the Lord's Prayer, Psalm 23, and the Ten Commandments; guidance in growing; ability to pray from the heart; becoming familiar with pledges of the American flag, the Christian flag, and the Bible; learning who the twelve disciples were; becoming familiar with the Old and New Testament comprising the sixty-six books of the Bible, as well as famous persons of the Bible; church etiquette; attendance at State Congress of Christian Education, the State Baptist Bible Camp, and the annual UBMEA Bible Camp; supporting all of Trinity's annual programs and events; striving for academic excellence; participating in oratorical contests sponsored by the Annual Congress of Christian Education and Annual Youth Day, second Sunday in June, which included recognition of graduates in the church family (high school, college, postgraduate, and so forth.) Awards were also given for high academic achievement, athletic achievement, and special recognition.

Workshops were conducted by specialists to talk about how-to topics: parliamentary procedure, how to fill out an application, how to develop phone etiquette, lessons in table etiquette and dining out. Trips were made available to expose youths to the arts: Tubman Museum, Disney World, and other events. They were taught the Ordinances of the Baptist Church. In 1987, the Baptist Youth Fellowship name was changed to Baptist Training Union.

Jesus and Me Ministry (JAMM)

The Jesus and Me Ministry (JAMM) began under the leadership of Anita Hogan. Its mission is simply to help our youth grow into a more intimate relationship with Christ through its regular JAMM sessions/Bible studies, outreach activities, praise and worship in all forms, prayer, and fellowship with other Christians, both young and old. Since its beginning, others contributed to make this ministry successful. They include Jessica Abrams, Talisha Moody, Kasey Swayne, Stephanie McBurrough, Carol Brown, Stephanie Freeman, Sabrina Brown, and Randell Hunt. Deacon Randell Hunt is presently serving as chairperson (2017).

The members are Schenericka Abrams, Laquinta Brown, Breonna Brown, Kiera Brown, Marquez Brown, Nykeema Burke, Lamaud Burden, Larry Burden, Hosea Carter, Chandris Fields, Dontrell Harris, Candy Jones, Johnny Jones, Oliver Lockett, Montana Mann, Saturn Mann, Addericka Meadows, Debarrius Miller, Isaiah Miller, Dnasis Miller, Ronnie Moody, Jr., Mary Grace Moore, William Moore, Justin Pearson, Ashley Pepper, Justin Plant, Shanequa Plant, Shavodus Plant, Braxton Postell, Devante Postell, Elreka Robinson, Talania Robinson, Catlin Small, Courtney Small, Ikea Smith, Jasmine Talton. Shnikea Talton, Nigel Talton, Keaya Turner, and Breona Wright.

Young Adult Ministry (YAM)

By First Lady Dr. Helen Louise Moore

First Lady Helen Louise Moore began working with Trinity's youths shortly after arriving at Trinity Baptist Church in 2001. She serves as director of the Young Adult Ministry (YAM). While working with the youths, she finds time to teach a Sunday school class for teens as well as direct plays and skits for the youth ministry. She has taught them the use of props and costumes to enhance the performances.

She introduced and trained the youths to perform human videos. This had not been done at the church or in the area at the time. The human video was performed to music with no props or words, using only their movements to tell the stories. First Lady Moore wrote, directed, choreographed, and staged many of the skits, scripts, and performances. She also developed a mime dance ministry at Trinity. It involves acting out a story through body movements and motion.

The youth performances gained recognition not only at Trinity, where they were asked regularly to participate in programs; they also gained recognition in other locations: Dublin, Reidsville, Perry, Warner Robins, various events in Fort Valley, and even Atlanta. Some of these events included Trinity's Candlelight Tea, Peach County Relay for Life, anniversaries, outreach festivals, and the Georgia Missionary Baptist Congress.

First Lady founded an abstinence ministry called "I'm Worth Waiting for, Are You?" She held many sessions presenting a curriculum for teaching abstinence to the church's teens. She was asked to speak at a conference and the Christian Student Fellowship organization at FVSU. Many, many teens and young adults were helped by following this curriculum. Several students gave testimony on how the ministry assisted them in living in purity. First Lady continued to present for several years with a successful all-day abstinence conference held at Trinity, with teens from local churches attending.

First Lady Moore also taught teen Bible study at JAMM (Jesus and Me Ministry) sessions. The lessons came from the International Sunday School Curriculum, her own lessons, and Bible study series requested by Pastor Gregory E. Moore. Worthy of mention, the teens joined the church in the study of Acts, chapters 1–25, in the spring of 2016. The classes were very well attended, with dinner served by the First Lady each week. The series culminated with a quiz bowl between the teen and adult Bible classes. The teen class gave a valiant effort, but the adult class emerged victorious.

She taught vacation Bible school classes and served as the health speaker for several years. She continues to work with the youths and teens and allows the Lord to use her in His service whenever possible. Listed below are titles from some of the skits and human video performances:

"Christmas and Sunday School"
"Everything"
"Am I Worth Dying For?"
"Break Every Chain"
"Do They Know It's Christmas"
"Oh, How He Loves Us"
"Holiday Helpline Crisis"
"Wise Men Don't Gripe"
"Season's Beatin's"
"Christmas Edition of *Family Feud*"
TWAR: "Trinity We Are Royalty"—Mime Ministry
"Better"
"Say Yes"

"God Is Here"
"Trinity Christmas Worship Service"
"Smile"

"Oh, What Love"

"Trinity Youth Rally"
"Relay for Life, Peach Medical Center"
"Chasing After You"
"He Wants It All"

"Praise Him in Advance"
"Trinity Father's Day"
"TWAR"—directed by LaJuan Martin

Chapter 7

THE INTERIM PERIOD, 1999–2000

Trust in the Lord with all thine heart … and He shall direct thy path.

—Proverbs 3:5–6 KJV

Elijah Weatherspoon, chairperson of the board of deacons, was ordained as deacon in 1978, along with John Thomas. He accepted his present role as chairperson after the resignation of Martin J. Edwards. Weatherspoon dedicated himself first to honoring God and to serving him in whatever capacity he was given. He served as a Sunday school teacher and was active in vacation Bible school activities, Ambassador Club, Chancel Choir, Troubadours; among other responsibilities, he accepted the duties of a sexton. He faithfully served as president and dean for the Congress of Christian Education, the Union Baptist Missionary, and the Educational Association of Middle Georgia, Inc. He was also given the honor of dean emeritus, Congress of Christian Education.

Following the death of Reverend Julius C. Simmons, Weatherspoon, as chairperson of the board of deacons, had the awesome job of keeping the congregation united. As moderator, he was responsible for conducting church conferences.

The June 1, 1999, church conference meeting was opened with an explanation of the purpose of the meeting and the task that lay before Trinity. He asked for unity during this ninety-day mourning period for Reverend Julius C. Simmons, pastor of Trinity Baptist Church for over forty years. "During this period," he stated, "no decisions will be made on calling a permanent pastor for Trinity. This time will be used to adjust, regroup, and assess where the church is and where the church needs to go.

This is a time an interim pastor is needed so that someone will be in place to conduct Sunday services and other activities and a search will not have to be done weekly."

Reverend Dr. Walter L. Glover, moderator of the Union Baptist Missionary and Educational Association of Middle Georgia, Inc., of which Trinity is a member, was invited to offer his assistance and to discuss other matters of importance, such as a need to select or call a pastor to serve during this crucial period. Reverend Dr. Glover stated while addressing the audience, "This is critical in the life of this church." He explained the need for an interim pastor and the protection this would give Trinity during its mourning period. He affirmed that he was ready to assist in whatever manner he could. He praised Trinity for showing concern for First Lady Simmons during this period. He also addressed the issue of selecting a search committee that represented every segment of the church: "The committee will not have the authority to call a minister; only the full active membership will have this authority." He cautioned, "Trinity should be sure to look for a person filled with the Holy Ghost, no matter how many educational degrees he holds. After the search process is completed and you are ready to recommend candidates, narrow the number to be presented. Do not hear so many—confusion will reign. Understand, whatever you do, whatever decision you make, do it prayerfully." The members asked Reverend Glover to assist in finding an interim pastor for Trinity.

Reverend Artha Grace, a local minister, offered his service and continued the worship service each Sunday. Reverend Grace had worked closely with Reverend Simmons during his tenure in the Fort Valley Ministerial Alliance.

> *And I will give you pastors according to mine heart,*
> *which shall feed you with knowledge and understanding.*
> --Jeremiah 3:15 KJV

The dutiful prayers were answered when Reverend Harry Harden accepted the position. Reverend Harry Harden of Macon, Georgia, was appointed as interim pastor of Trinity Baptist Church, Fort Valley, Georgia, in June 1999. His strong spiritual leadership and guidance skills moved Trinity forward into the new millennium.

Reverend Harry Harden had served previously as associate pastor at the Mount Olive Baptist Church, Macon, Georgia, and pastor of the Springfield Baptist Church, Rome, Georgia. He was educated in the public schools of Bibb County. He studied at the Christian College of Georgia and received bachelor's and master's degrees in

Spanish from the University of Georgia, Athens, Georgia, and a degree in guidance and counseling from Fort Valley State University, Fort Valley, Georgia.

He showed his love for the congregation and was received by all who encountered him. He worked diligently during his short tenure in preparation for Trinity's eighty-eighth church anniversary, scheduled for January 23, 2000. He preached the morning worship sermon at the eleven o'clock hour, not knowing that this was his goodbye message. At the end of the service, while greeting the worshippers leaving the church, he collapsed. Dr. Luther Vance, MD, a member of Trinity from Perry, Georgia, rushed to his side. He was taken by ambulance to the Peach County Regional Hospital, Fort Valley, Georgia, where he never regained consciousness and died at 2:27 p.m. The church family was stunned. Reverend Henry C. Ficklin, Mount Vernon Baptist Church, was invited as guest speaker for the afternoon program. Reverend Ficklin preached to an extremely sad and grieving audience.

Reverend Harry Harden, Interim Pastor, 1999-2000

Harry Harden

The following is a tribute to the late Reverend Harry Harden in honor of his work at Trinity Baptist Church, written by Barbara H. Palmer (2000).

"The Harden Report" (unpublished)

I did the best I could at Trinity. I was available to the membership. I prepared sermons, carrying lessons on, living the good life. My themes, either explicit or implicit, ranged from giving freely, respect, honor, humbleness, faith, hope, service, and feeding the hungry to love of God, family, and friends.

I tried to serve as a living testimony of all the characteristics I just mentioned and more. On the subject of love, I told them, as you taught, that love suffers long and is kind, and love does not envy. Love does not parade itself, is not puffed up, does not behave rudely, does not seek its own, is not easily provoked, and thinks no evil. I sought to demonstrate this definition by developing a loving and caring relationship with the membership. I knew everybody by name, from Ikeia and Elijah to Sister Alice Davis. I greeted each worshipper after church. I visited the sick and called to check on members who were undergoing trials in their lives. I stressed love of and support for the church, no matter who happened to be the leader.

I rejoiced in the success of others. I especially praised the young people and rewarded them for their good work. I admonished the members to be supportive and praised them too. I remained humble. I remembered my roots; many times, I told my story of growing up in Macon, Georgia, of Mama and others in the family. I told them how Ms. Ruby came by and took care of me during my seven months of illness.

I tried to get the membership involved in service. I wanted them to get busy doing your will, Lord.

I preached about hope and spreading the Word. I urged them to seek out members … and tell them God is calling you and God loves you.

His sudden death brought comments from many of Trinity's members: "He must have been God sent." "He came and did what God wanted him to do." "We were so complacent and content under Reverend Simmons that Reverend Harden put us to work." "We were like his schoolchildren, glad to do whatever task he assigned us." During his six-month tenure at Trinity, his emphasis to the members was from a biblical passage in the book of James: "Faith without works is dead" (James 2:26 KJV).

On March 5, 2000, the black-draped chair in the pulpit and the door symbols denoting the death of Reverend Harden were removed. A moment of silent prayer was given as the congregation silently wept and relived his memory at Trinity Baptist Church.

Reverend Joseph Rumph, a native Fort Valleyan, was asked to serve as interim pastor of Trinity Baptist Church. Reverend Rumph remained for a brief period before announcing his resignation. A church conference was called on June 9, 2001, to address his request and resignation. Elijah Weatherspoon, conference moderator, addressed the audience and read a petition addressed to the board of deacons from an unnamed group of members. The moderator explained that the board of deacons met with the group but no action had been taken. He continued, saying that the first item of concern was for another interim pastor to replace Reverend Rumph, who resigned in June of 2001 with ill feelings toward Trinity. A motion was given that "within thirty days of the date of this conference, the board of deacons should issue a formal written expression to Reverend Joseph Rumph, which states unequivocal gratitude for services rendered as interim pastor." It also stated that the letter should offer a formal apology for any incidents, conditions, or circumstances, intentional or unintentional, from any sources [that] may have cast even a shadow of unpleasantness during his tenure." The motion further stated that "copies of the letter should be issued to chairs of auxiliaries and read at the next conference." The motion called for discussion since some attendees were unaware of what caused the distress. The response was that "because he felt that he had been mistreated, an apology should be issued to him, hoping to clear up any perceived unpleasantness." After some discussion, a substitute motion was made that the letter addressed to Reverend Joseph Rumph incorporate the words "From the Trinity Baptist Church family and not the deacon board." The motion was seconded and passed.

Prior to Reverend Harden's death, a pastor search committee was commissioned by the congregation at a church conference, November 20, 1999, to perform the most profound and reverent task our church has ever been confronted with—to begin a search, to screen, and to recommend a candidate or candidates to become our pastor. Thirteen members were entrusted with the task of seeking a successor to Reverend Julius C. Simmons, who passed into eternal rest in May of 1999. They included Inez Brewton, David Eaton, John Demons, Gloria Harris, Mary Huggins, Wilmetta Jackson, Lillian Kimbro, Clifford Ponder, Denise Small, Sabastian Walker, Annie Pearl Wilkerson, Alice Mathis, and Leonard Arnold Giles, Jr. The committee conducted many closed sessions at Camp John Hope to pray, meditate, and ask God for guidance in helping them faithfully fulfill the task assigned to them.

The pastor search committee conducted its first meeting. John Demons was elected chairperson. One of the first steps taken by the search committee in an effort to fulfill their obligation was to prepare a handbook titled "Trinity Baptist Church Profile" to guide them through the process.

The pastor search committee called a special conference on October 9, 2000, to conduct one item of business: extending a call to a prospective pastor. John Demons, chairperson, addressed the congregation and announced that he was making a nondebatable motion: "Brother Moderator, on behalf of the search committee, I move that Reverend Lorenza Davis be called as our pastor. This call is based on salary and benefits approved by our church in the business session on Saturday, September 23, 2000, and the minister-church agreement approved on Saturday, September 23, 2000. This motion carries no changes or request for changes that differ from what was approved on above or forestated date."

This motion caused a discussion on the lack of parliamentary procedures by making a nondebatable motion. Elijah Weatherspoon, conference moderator, explained why this type of motion was used and said that the recommended wording of the motion was taken from a guide called "Pastor and Staff Search Committee Guide," by Don R. Mathis, used by the committee. The voting process proceeded. A special conference on October 15, 2000, was called to give the results of the vote. The candidate, Reverend Lorenza Davis, was defeated with a vote of forty-eight to forty-one.

A conference was held on June 9, 2001. Clifford Ponder, cochairperson, gave the pastor search committee report. He shared information concerning the steps and procedures used in searching for and screening of candidates to become the pastor of Trinity Baptist Church. Ponder recommended that procedures currently in place be changed so that instead of presenting one candidate at a time to the congregation, the committee would present all recommended at one time so that the church membership would have choices in making the selection. A motion was made and passed. It was suggested that the candidates be allowed to preach at least twice (back-to-back) when presented. The committee also announced that there would be three candidates recommended for the hearing. Information about each candidate would be given to the congregation before the person was presented, and a time would be set aside for interaction with the candidate.

Following the report from the committee, a motion was made from the floor, indicating that it was the consensus that too much time had been taken to find a pastor for Trinity and that the committee had shared not enough information. The motion read, "I move that the current pastoral search committee be recalled, decommissioned, and dissolved, and a new committee be selected or elected. Further, we want the new committee to be comprised of seven duly selected or elected members at this June ninth church conference." After hearing the pro and con discussions, the motion was withdrawn.

On August 12, 2001, during the Sunday morning worship service, Reverend J. H. Flakes, Sr., pastor, Fourth Street Baptist Church, Columbus, Georgia, and president of the State Congress of Christian Education was invited to preach to the congregation. His subject was "Under the Leadership of the Holy Spirit." Prior to Reverend Flakes's message, he distributed copies of his sermon and gave instructions to the congregation that this information be read in unison and led by him.

Following the worship hour, with all minds clearly focused on the sermon, the moderator announced the convening of a special conference to hear a report given by John Demons, chairperson of the pastor search committee. The report offered a motion that the process of voting on a pastor begin at this meeting according to guidelines set forth by the conference on August 2, 2001. It was moved, seconded, and passed. The candidates presented were Reverend Lenorris Dixon, Albany, Georgia; Reverend Timothy Reed, Atlanta, Georgia; and Reverend Gregory Moore, Hawkinsville, Georgia.

The voting process began by having each individual stand for the candidate of their choice as the name was called and remain standing until the counting was completed. At the end, a motion was made, seconded, and passed. The call was extended to Reverend Gregory Moore, Hawkinsville, Georgia, who had the most votes, to become the leader as pastor of Trinity Baptist Church.

After the voting, the church covenant was read. The moderator and Reverend Flakes gave their closing remarks and prayer.

Chapter 8

A MAN WITH A MESSAGE: "EXPECT GREAT THINGS FROM GOD ..."

—Reverend Gregory E. Moore

I am crucified with Christ: nevertheless I live; yet not I, but Christ liveth in me.

—Galatians 2:20 KJV

Personal Background

Pastor Gregory Emille Moore, a young, energetic man of God, received the call to pastor at Trinity Missionary Baptist Church as its seventeenth pastor. Pastor Moore was born in Douglas, Georgia. He attended Coffee High School, where he played the trumpet in the band and was on the varsity baseball team. He attended Georgia Southwestern College, Americus, Georgia, to complete prerequisites to attend the Medical College of Georgia in Augusta. He participated in marching, concert, theater, and jazz bands while at Georgia Southwestern. He served on the student government at both schools and as the president of the Student Medical Technology Association at the Medical College of Georgia. He graduated in 1991 with a bachelor of science degree in medical technology. Pastor Moore worked in the chemistry laboratory of the Department of Pathology at the Medical College of Georgia for eight years.

Pastor Moore attended Macedonia Baptist Church while in Augusta. It was there, in December of 1993, that he received his calling to the ministry under the mentorship of Reverend J.S. Wright. At Macedonia, he worked diligently as a Sunday school teacher, youth minister, associate minister, and as a member of the male chorus. As youth minister, he coordinated the children's church and developed a successful Bible memorization program, where students were rewarded at certain points in their progress. He planned and conducted the first Macedonia youth retreat for teenage members, where students were challenged to stand for Christ despite peer pressure.

During this time, he met and married his wife, Dr. Helen-Louise Williams Moore, a native of Columbus, Georgia. Dr. Helen-Louise W. Moore is a pediatrician at Pediatric Associates and Pediatric Associates South, Warner Robins, Georgia. They have three children, William Gregory Moore, Helen Mary Grace Moore, and Christiana Moore.

Pastor Moore attended Columbia Biblical Seminary, where he earned a master of divinity degree in 1998. In June 1999, he and his family relocated to Athens, Georgia, where they joined and attended Ebenezer Baptist Church, where Dr. Winfred Hope is pastor. He was director of Christian Education Ministry at Ebenezer. He worked diligently to increase attendance in Bible study, also recruiting, enlisting, and training Sunday school teachers. He also served as an adult Sunday school teacher, Bible study teacher, and associate minister.

In December of 2014, Pastor Moore received a doctorate from the Southern Baptist Theological Seminary in Louisville, Kentucky. His dissertation was "Developing and Implementing a Discipleship Curriculum for Young Adult Men at Trinity Baptist Church."

Leadership and Administration

In January 2000, he and his family moved to Hawkinsville, Georgia. In August 2001, he received the call to pastor at Trinity Missionary Baptist Church. In a statement, he wrote, "I am humbled that the Holy Spirit has seen fit to join me with Trinity Baptist Church for the work and the glory of God. With great joy, I accept this pastoral position and all the blessings and hardships that will pertain to it."

Reverend Moore's leadership and dedication have had an impact on the congregation as well as the community. His accomplishments include changing the church's outside appearance with the installation of a church steeple, also adding a new heating and air-conditioning unit as well as a marquee built to house the original bell removed from the bell tower. He reorganized and initiated new ministries for youths, teenagers, senior members, the Children's Church Ministry, the FVSU Outreach Ministry, and the Seasoned Saints Ministry. He encouraged the congregation to become involved in prayer teams, praying for those requesting prayer, providing clothing for those in need with the annual picnic/clothing giveaway, and praising God in all we do through the Praise Team and Julius C. Simmons Gospel Choir.

Pastor Moore is an excellent teacher. His Bible study class has drawn men and women from other churches in Fort Valley. He has initiated an orientation class for new members. He is the author of two books: *Ready to Teach Bible Studies: 52 Bible Studies for the Entire Year* and *What God Expects of Every Christian*. The latter book is used to orient new members by guiding them through a study of ten core lessons essential for Christianity. He provides Christian Education class 101 and Christology 102. He conducts various other classes and workshops to encourage and train new teachers as to effectively teaching the Bible, to train deacons on conflict resolution, and to train many on the practice of sharing scripture with others and various other topics he presents in Bible study classes. He also leads Bible study at venues in the local and surrounding community that have a room available for rent once a week. He invites lecturers to share inspiring and informative messages on Christian living and church growth. He also initiated the purchase and finance of a bus by the church, with a commitment from each member to make monthly payments of forty dollars with their tithing until the total amount was paid off.

Pastor Moore continues to encourage his congregation, pouring his heart into training members for discipleship and engaging them to make disciples for Christ. He acknowledges and praises God for everything he does, realizing that "Without God, man can do nothing" (John 15:5 KJV). He makes himself available by scheduling office hours for three days a week. Lillian Kimbro serves as secretary.

Vision

His vision has included the expansion and building of a new sanctuary. A committee under the leadership of Dr. William D. Moorehead, chairperson of the building committee, secured the services of Ackey & Associates Architectural Firm of Macon, Georgia, to develop a design for a new sanctuary. The plans were approved by the

Chapter 9

SERVICE OF INSTALLATION, 2001

Greater is He that is in me than he that is in the world.

—1 John 4:4 KJV

Pastor's Pen

I am humbled that the Holy Spirit has seen fit to join me with Trinity Baptist Church for the work and the glory of God. This is the fruition of answered prayer on behalf of the members of Trinity and myself. With great joy, I accept this pastoral position and all the blessings and hardships that will follow. I come with the confidence that God always guides and sustains both shepherd and flock. With God on our side, there is nothing and no one for us to fear. Knowing this, let us march on with our heads up, chests out, and eyes stayed on Jesus! We must never cease to acknowledge this truth: "Greater is He that is in me than he that is in the world" 1 John 4:4 KJV.

I love the gospel ministry. I have had the opportunity to pursue several different careers and have found that the only work that brings the joy and satisfaction I desire in life is the gospel ministry; thus I know that God has called me to this work. I enjoy seeing how the various ministries of the gospel bless so many lives. Teaching the gospel helps others to grow in knowledge, faith, and application of God's word. Preaching the gospel message reassures the believer, pricks the heart of the unrepentant, and glorifies the name of the Father. Counseling with the Word provides a setting for a more personal sharing of the healing power that can address ungodly behavior and encourage righteousness in personal difficulties. Church administration based on the goal of salvation allocates funds and tailors planning to keep the church in line with the will of God. Biblical leadership and stewardship teach members to walk the walk after the teaching, preaching, counseling, and administering have been put into place. The gospel ministry has brought great joy in my life from infancy until the present time and by faith assuredly for the eternity of time. It has loved and cared for me, and I have learned to love and be responsible to it.

In summary, Ephesians 4:11–12 KJV reveals God's intentions for pastors to equip church members to become disciples who in turn make more disciples. This requires extensive and continuous training. I intend to devote a great deal of time to training and seeking training for all laypersons. Trinity must use the spiritual gifts of this membership fully. All members will be encouraged to work in areas where their gifts will be of greatest benefit to the kingdom of God.

Trinity, as well as myself, must understand that I am God's servant above all and am here to do His will. I have not come to Trinity to become comfortable or to make the membership comfortable with the status quo. In Acts 5:29, the apostles make it clear that "it is better to obey God than to obey man." We must be careful that our will takes a back seat to the will of God.

My vision for Trinity is to become a church where membership is synonymous with discipleship; where evangelism is not a special effort but a way of life; where Bible study assures, encourages, challenges, and convicts; where worship is filled with the joyful noise of praise; and where prayer and supplication go on without ceasing. Let us do this to the extent that we become like a maternity ward where new Christians are born every day, cared for by a well-trained discipleship staff.

This vision will come with a price. It has been said that salvation is free but the gospel ministry is expensive. We must be prepared to sacrificially offer our time, talents, and treasure to a greater degree than we have in the past. If we do not become weary in well-doing, God will reward us in due time. Let us look forward to both the work and the promise of God's reward. Expect great things from God but also attempt great things for God.

I bring with me to Trinity a loving wife (Helen-Louise), a son (William, three years), and a daughter (Mary-Grace, ten months). God holds me responsible for their care and well-being above all else. Scripture makes this known in 1 Timothy 3:5 KJV: "For if a man does not know how to rule his own household, how is he to take care of the church of God?" I ask your prayers for the Spirit to strengthen and maintain the loving bond that holds my family together. We are excited to have a new church family and church home where we can worship and grow together. We can only do this as we maintain a strong bond of familial love.

Finally, my Christian testimony can be summed up with this passage in Galatians 2:20: "I have been crucified with Christ, yet it is no longer I who live but Christ lives in me." Christ's residence in my life is what has brought me here to Trinity. He began His work in me through the faithfulness of my parents, who, before their passage into glory, instilled in me the love of Jesus Christ. Jesus began this work in me, and I glory in the fact that he will finish it. He has promised and is indeed with us all, even until the end of the world.

Chapter 10

CELEBRATE GOD'S FAITHFULNESS TO TRINITY

Ninetieth Church Anniversary

January 27, 2002

Pastor's Pen

Rejoice, be glad, and celebrate ninety years of God's faithfulness to Trinity Missionary Baptist Church. For ninety years, He has landed us safely on the other side of every river we have had to cross. No doubt God has done many great things for us. We must continue to attempt to do great things for Him. Make it a part of your life's daily routine to witness about His gospel and to be an active participant in ministering to those in need. These are great things in the eyes of God.

Our task is always to join together as one body and to use every gift, every talent, and every resource at our disposal to loudly magnify the Lord our God. Be an unswerving believer that God has given the church the power to transform communities and the world. He has not given us a spirit of fear but one of great heavenly power. Rise up and march on until the victory is won! Let's be steadfast in prayer and fasting that God will empower us to do His will. Afterward, let us be obedient to His will. The Lord has been faithful to us for ninety years; there is no reason to doubt him now. He has promised to be with us even unto the end of the world.

Chapter 11

WE HAVE HEARD, NOW LET US DO

—James 1:22 KJV

Ninety-First Church Anniversary
January 26, 2003

Pastor's Pen

Let us give all praise and glory to God for ninety-one years of faithfulness and provision to the Trinity Baptist Missionary Church. We thank God foremost for the maintenance of our spiritual relationship with Him. He is always doing something great to let us know that He is and will always be with us through good times and bad. Such faithfulness maintains the cheerfulness of our spirits. Let us also praise Him for ninety-one years of answering the prayers of our sick, lonely, heartbroken, and the new believers he has rescued from the penalty of eternal death. The Lord has and continues to provide finances beyond our needs. By His blessings, we have been able to maintain and purchase all the materials and structures we need to carry out His ministry. We can be confident that He will provide again when the time comes.

We are thankful to God for faithful and committed members over the years. Many who have passed on went beyond the call of duty to help make Trinity what it is today. Past pastors, Sunday school teachers, deacons, trustees, choir members, ushers, and all other participants have passed to us a great opportunity to continue the ministry of the Lord. Let's see to it that their sacrifices yield much fruit.

In the ninety-first year, we are going to put more effort into outreach to youth and young adults through children's church and the FVSU Ministries. In a culture where youth and young adults are inundated with negative messages from rap music, movies, and talk shows, we must present the more attractive and clearly superior alternative of a Christian life and message.

I call upon all members this year to work to strengthen our personal relationship with the Lord. The strength of the entire church body is dependent upon the strength of each member. If you want Trinity to become stronger, don't look outward but inward.

Our motto for 2003 is "We Have Heard, Now Let Us Do" (James 1:22 KJV). After ninety-one years of preaching, teaching, praying, and worshipping, we should be ready to carry out the work God has called us to do. This is not a time to slow down but rather to speed up our efforts for the kingdom. God has given us our marching orders. If we are obedient to Him, He will also give us the power of resources to carry them out. As we have for ninety-one years, let us continue to walk by faith and not by sight (2 Corinthians 5:7).

Chapter 12

PASSING THE BATON OF FAITH

—Matthew 5:16 KJV

Ninety-Second Church Anniversary
January 25, 2004

Pastor's Pen

As usual and as expected, God has shown himself to be faithful in Trinity for another year. Let us join together in sending up songs, prayers, service, and shouts of praise. It has been ninety-two years since Trinity was established, and the Lord has never left us nor forsaken us. For ninety-two years, He has cleansed us, saved us, healed us, empowered us, encouraged us, protected us, and made every provision we have needed to carry out the great commission of spreading the gospel and for living lives of spiritual abundance.

Our theme for 2004 is "Passing the Baton of Faith." It is based on the scripture passage found in Matthew 5:16 KJV: "Let your light so shine before men, that they may see your good works, and glorify your Father which is in Heaven." What have you learned about being a Christian? How much has your relationship with the Lord grown over the years? What wisdom have you acquired during your life of studying Christianity? Take all of that and be determined to pass it ("baton of faith") on to someone else this year. It could be to a new believer, an unbeliever, a mature Christian, a family member, a young or old person, a church member, or a non–church member. All believers have the responsibility to pass on what they have learned. We can no longer afford to allow secular views to be passed on more effectively than those of the Christian faith. Ways of life that are not for God are against God. If we want to live in godly communities, we must be serious about the business of passing on godliness. If all we do is wrap our arms around others and say "Jesus Loves You," then let us be determined to do it with a passion unheard of in our community. If we do this, we ensure that Trinity will run with the baton of faith for another ninety-two years.

Please pray for the spiritual success of the newly restructured youth ministry. The staff and kids need your help and prayers. We must present our youth with the kind of lives God has chosen for them in response to so many poor and shameful examples they get from the media, streets, and other communication outlets. Pray also for the Seasoned Saints Ministry. If we do everything well and yet forget to honor those who have been on the battlefield for the Lord through many seasons, then there will always be an empty spot in our heart. We must remember those who were pillars for Trinity through good and bad times. I say to all our Seasoned Saints, thank you! We would not be where we are had it not been for your sacrifice.

I am excited about what the Lord will do at Trinity this year. God be willing, we will immediately begin office hours with a staff of pastor and secretary, train new teachers to teach God's Word in various capacities, receive lecturers who will share inspiring and informative lectures on Christian living and church growth, purchase a new church bus, move forward in our expansion planning, celebrate a FVSU student and faculty day, and the list goes on and on. Suffice it to say, we have much work ahead of us so roll up your sleeves and set your mind on the tasks that will bring glory to the Lord in 2004.

Chapter 13

THE PRAYER OF THE RIGHTEOUS AVAILETH MUCH

––James 5:16b KJV

Ninety-Third Church Anniversary
January 23, 2005

Pastor's Pen

Let us all join in a great shout of praise to the Lord for ninety-three years of faithfulness to the members of Trinity Missionary Baptist Church. His Spirit, working in the members of Trinity, has kept us alive and strong over the years. Oh! Thanks be to God, who has given us the victory over every circumstance so that we can continue being a light for Him. Let us seek always to do His will until the day He calls us from labor to reward.

The church is the body of Christ called to bring glory to one God in many ways. God has gifted every member of Trinity to make a dynamic and extraordinary contribution to the edification of the church body. Have you been using yours? The expression of gifts results in the difference between being a stationary (serving self-interest) and a missionary (on the move for God) Baptist Church. Let us commit to not only be organized for God but to being a living organism for Him.

The Lord has truly blessed Trinity over the past year. We have been able to pay off our van and the church mortgage. We've been blessed to purchase a church bus with no bank financing; put church services on attractive CDs; begin Wednesday noon Bible study; and complete *Effective Bible Teaching* training, which has yielded six additional Bible teachers, with five more in training this year. We've added more members to our prayer teams and have begun two new Sunday school classes targeting our young men and women: Phenomenal Women of God and Young Men of God. God is doing great things at Trinity, and He is just getting started.

James 5:16b KJV tells us "the prayer of the righteous availeth much." With this in mind, I ask that you pray for the following concerns for this year: establishment of a church nursery, development of our youth choir, that the Building and Expansion Committee continues to make much progress, increase Sunday school attendance, and continued spiritual growth for all the members of Trinity. Finally, please, for the pastor, ask the Lord to give me pastoral wisdom and a fire for the work of the ministry. Pray that He will continue my spiritual growth because I can lead you only as far as He carries me.

Now let us ready our hands, feet, hearts, minds, spirits, and resources for the exciting work God has for us this year. We need only to seek the kingdom of heaven first (Matthew 6:33 KJV) and all these other things will be provided for us. Glory to God in the highest!

Chapter 14

LIGHT TO THE COMMUNITY

––Matthew 5:16 KJV

Ninety-Fourth Church Anniversary
January 22, 2006

Pastor's Pen

All honor and praise be to God for ninety-four years of faithfulness to the members of Trinity Missionary Baptist Church. We owe it all to Him! Can there be any doubt that only by the grace of God we are where we are today? From Adam and Eve to the present generation, the Lord has been a great and mighty God to all of His people. Truly, He loves us all and burns with a passion to see all come to repentance of their sins and receive Jesus Christ as their Lord and Savior.

We've had our share of sickness, death, pain, and mourning this year, but none of it has been able to separate us from the love of God. In every circumstance, He provided the healing, power, love, deliverance, comfort, and strength we needed to carry on and indeed go to higher heights. Trials work for our good when we see God working through them. We must remember that troubles come to make us strong and rocks help us to climb mountains. From them, we learn to trust in Jesus and depend upon His promises of faithfulness. Because of this, we've been able to persevere for ninety-four years.

Let's join together and make 2006 a grand year of being a "Light to the Community" for Jesus Christ. We want to compel men, women, boys, and girls to choose Christ on an unprecedented scale. This is the difference between "coming" to church and actually "being" the church. I pray that every ministry will gird up their courage and determination to target some event or place in the community where they may make an impact for Christ. My prayer is that every member, on an individual basis, will take a personal interest in shining the light of Christ in some area of darkness in Peach County. This is the call and commission of Jesus to us all. In very clear terms, He calls us to "Let our lights so shine before men that they will see our good works and glorify God in heaven" (Matthew 5:16 KJV). He has already guaranteed victory if we will be obedient to go. We can rejoice every day knowing that light always overpowers darkness. All we have to do is just let it shine! Let it shine! Let it shine!

Finally, we must improve on and continue to do those things that keep Trinity strong. They include studying the Word, coming to Bible study and Sunday school, being faithful and generous in giving tithes and offerings, praying without end, being tireless in service, having love for everyone, forgiving one another, and being steadfast and unmovable where Christian standards are concerned. If we are obedient in doing these things, nothing can stop us from making a spiritual impact in our community. Can the Lord count on Trinity to be as faithful to Him as He has been to Trinity for ninety-four years? Let our response be a resounding "Certainly, certainly, certainly, Lord!"

Chapter 15

BEING AN EXTRAORDINARY CHURCH IN EXTRAORDINARY TIMES

Ninety-Fifth Church Anniversary
January 28, 2007

Pastor's Pen

Thanks be to God for ninety-five years of faithfulness to the Trinity Church Family. By the power of His Spirit, the Lord has brought us over every mountain and through every valley. All that we have done, both small and large, must be attributed to Him. When we meet together, there should be great worship and praise in His honor. Our God is indeed an awesome God and more than worthy of being praised.

In response to God's faithfulness, Trinity needs to show its faithfulness to Him. Let's expect great things from God but also attempt great things for God. Let's be a light in our community for Christ, who has blessed us with His light in our lives.

Our theme this year is "Being an Extraordinary Church in Extraordinary Times." Can anyone deny that we serve a God who is an extraordinary God in extraordinary times? We have all had our extraordinary times, and every time God proved Himself to be the extraordinary God we needed in those times. The Father is extraordinary. The Son is extraordinary. The Holy Spirit is extraordinary. If they all live inside of us, shouldn't we be an extraordinary church? It would not be a good testimony to proclaim that an extraordinary God lives within us yet practice only ordinary Christianity. Let's commit ourselves to being an extraordinary church in extraordinary times.

How do we become extraordinary? First, we need to admit that the level of immorality and darkness in our community is alarming. Admitting this helps us to see the need and gets us primed to be the kind of light that is needed to make a spiritual impact in our community. Second, we need to increase our standards for personal growth. Studying the Bible, attending Bible study, fervent prayer, passionate praise, fasting, daily worship, and quiet time with the Lord must become daily activities. Ministries must seek to go beyond what they have ordinarily done or at least do what they have been doing in an extraordinary way. We must cry out to Christ for a miraculous move of the Spirit to break the bondage of the ordinary. Pray for new hearts, new excitement, new commitment, new joy, and love that passes all understanding. Then be a leader in living out these characteristics.

To be extraordinary means we must be united. We can't let petty differences divide us. Ordinary churches are easily divided; extraordinary churches are not! Spreading the gospel of Christ is our central mission. All other administration is just side orders.

Pray for Trinity to grow in spirit and in members. Petition the Lord to heal our sick and comfort our lonely and mourning. Ask Him to anoint every leader in Trinity to help carry the heavy load in an extraordinary way. Make passionate supplications to the Lord to help us implement our building and expansion plans and to give us great financial increase to exceed all expenses.

If we fast and pray fervently for all these concerns, something extraordinary is going to happen at Trinity. If we don't allow ourselves to be divided, something extraordinary is going to happen at Trinity. Something is going to happen that maybe hasn't happened in ninety-five years. If we commit ourselves to serving God in an extraordinary way, He will make us an extraordinary church in these extraordinary times. Believe it! Expect it! Get ready to receive it!

Chapter 16

BUILDING THE KINGDOM THROUGH "INREACH" AND OUTREACH

Ninety-Seventh Church Anniversary
January 25, 2009

Pastor's Pen

God has once again shown His faithfulness to Trinity for another year. Give Him glory and praise. Every year for ninety-seven years, God has provided for all of our spiritual and material needs. He has ministered to us individually and as a church body.

Anything that lasts for ninety-seven years and is still going strong has a great Maker. We have the greatest Maker in the universe, and we should be proud to tell others how great He is. To a certain extent, we should not be surprised, because the Lord did say, "Upon this rock I will build my church and the gates of hell shall not prevail against it" (Matthew 16:18 KJV). After ninety-seven years, we should be convinced that it is God who sustains the church. All praises be to His holy name.

Our theme for this year is "Building the Kingdom through 'Inreach' and Outreach." My prayer is that this theme will help us focus on our total mission. We don't want to do one and let the other go undone. We must grow within and outside the church walls. Let us grow by both reaching in and reaching out.

Reaching in requires us to engage in acts of discipleship. This includes making the time to fellowship with one another and encouraging each other through prayer and Christian counseling, excellence in Bible teaching, dynamic praise and worship, and having hearts that are quick to forgive, slow to anger, and overflowing in love. Outreach demands that we put together a plan and execute a strategy to impact our local community with the gospel through meeting a need, establishing relationships, helping service organizations, and sharing the gospel as a daily routine.

We have a plan in place through our Community Evangelistic Outreach Ministry (CEOs). Please receive them in love, as they have been charged with helping all of our ministries to be connected with some community organization where they can shine the light of Christ through their Christian service. Pray fervently that God will anoint this effort.

Remember that our purpose, both individually and corporately, is to glorify God in all that we do. Romans 11:36 KJV tells us that all things are to be for God's glory. Be sure your motive for all you do is for God's glory. This is the only way you will be able to continue serving in difficult times.

Acts 2:42–47 KJV gives a vivid picture of how the first church was saturated in Christian fellowship. I believe the contemporary church has lost this fellowship and we should work to restore it. Make it your goal this year, perhaps after worship service, to spend some time fellowshipping with your fellow church members. Can a family that spends no time together really be called a family? Let's take the time and effort to be the church family God wants us to be.

Please fast and pray that God will make us successful in building His kingdom in 2009. When you fast, turn off all media, avoid friends and the telephone, and try to avoid going out in public. It is a time to focus completely on the Lord. If you can't fast for medical reasons, find something else to set aside. Read your Bible, play gospel music, and most of all, pray as much as you can. If we all do this, expect God to do great miracles at Trinity this year!

Chapter 17

MAKING DISCIPLES BY LOVING GOD AND LOVING PEOPLE

Ninety-Eighth Church Anniversary
January 2010

Pastor's Pen

Discipleship ensures there will always be leaders for the church of the future. It is vital to the continued spiritual and numerical growth and the survival for every church. It is the way we replenish the church with workers for the harvest. Thus we must disciple and seek to do it well.

Trinity has been around for ninety-eight years because each generation of disciples took upon themselves the task of discipling another generation. Every year the discipleship process continues at Trinity to ensure that we will remain in a place where people are equipped to do the work of Christ in the Fort Valley community.

Our motivation for making disciples comes from our love for God and for people. In Matthew 22:37–39 KJV, Jesus taught that the greatest commandment is to love God with all our hearts, minds, and souls, and furthermore to love our neighbors in the way we love ourselves. Our theme this year is "Making Disciples by Loving God and Loving People." Love is the most powerful force within us, and when it is the motivation for our discipleship, we disciple with passion, commitment, and an unquenchable determination to see others come to Christ and grow in Christ. Let us give God our best effort.

Even though love may be our most powerful motivator, discipleship doesn't happen by chance. It takes a firm commitment to sacrifice the time to do it. It takes a mind committed to coming up with creative and innovative ways to teach and fellowship with those we seek to serve. It takes a passionate desire to see the plans for discipleship put into action. All these attributes, along with love, are a guaranteed winning combination.

Discipleship is what we are committing ourselves to doing this year and every year because the commandment (Matthew 28:18–20 KJV) Christ gave us to make disciples is new every day. I am asking Trinity to joyfully join in the planning process of discovering how we can best develop others and ourselves into more effective disciples for Christ. May every ministry at Trinity consider what it can do to help new and established members grow in spiritual maturity. The future effectiveness and existence of Trinity depends upon our discipleship efforts today.

The most encouraging aspect of this entire discipleship effort is glaring simplicity. New and established members simply want to be loved and included in fellowship. Many people are just looking for one true friend. The question is, who's going to be that friend to reach out and sacrifice the time, commitment, and love to embrace those who need a relationship with Christ? My prayer is that every member of Trinity will answer, "I *will*!" If we give this answer, God will someday give the response "Well done!"

Chapter 18

BUILDING A BIGGER BOAT TO BRING IN A BIGGER CATCH FOR CHRIST

Trinity's One Hundredth Church Anniversary
January 2012

Pastor's Pen

Beloved brethren and sisters, we are celebrating one hundred years of God's faithfulness to Trinity Baptist Church. God has continued to pour out His Spirit of divine inspiration on each generation of Trinity members to pass the baton of faith to the next generation. Many of our past members did not live to see this day, but the Lord has blessed us to be here to witness and celebrate this momentous landmark in our history. Let us lift up our voices and be glad—and let our tongues be saturated with words, songs, and prayers of thanksgiving! Tell your family members, friends, colleagues, and neighbors that God has sustained us as a Christian family for one hundred years!

One hundred years of existence would not have been possible without members who were faithful and committed to carrying out the will and the ministry of the Lord through the decades. Our patriarchs and matriarchs held up the cross of Christ through segregation, injustice, and inequality. How much more should we be able to do today now that we have many more opportunities in education, civil freedoms, and access to gainful employment? Through it all, they maintained an optimistic outlook, faithfulness in service, faithfulness in giving, faithfulness in prayer, and faithfulness in worship. Let us build on their Christian legacy by continuing to be faithful in Christian disciplines and innovative in Christian outreach strategies.

It brings me great joy to know that we are preparing the way to continue God's ministry into the next century as we are diligently raising funds and planning to build our new sanctuary. I am proud of the slogan we have adopted to rally around: "Building a Bigger Boat to Bring in a Bigger Catch For Christ." What better reason to build a new sanctuary than to expand our facilities expressly to increase our service, outreach, and discipleship of new believers for Christ? Matthew 6:33 KJV says, "Seek ye first the kingdom of heaven and his righteousness and all these other things shall be added unto thee." As we keep the will of God first, God will do signs and wonders that we could have never imagined. He will give us success.

The future of Trinity is bright and full of divine potential. Let us go forward with a spirit of great expectation that the Lord will honor our efforts through blessings that we can use to bless him further again. Be a part of the next century by participating in every way possible, fasting and praying, trusting God's direction and intervention for success, and stepping out on faith. The Lord has sustained us for one hundred years, and he will be faithful to do the same in this next century. Be encouraged! Amen!

Chapter 19

TRINITY'S 101ST CHURCH ANNIVERSARY

January 2013

Pastor's Pen

Praise be to God for our 101st church anniversary! The power of His Spirit has sustained this church family for over a century and no doubt will continue to sustain us until He returns to take us back with Him. Oh, what shall we render unto God for all the good things He has done for us? Let us give Him our most humble service, most sacrificial gift, and our most unrestrained praise!

This year our theme is "Reaching People by Meeting People." Before we can reach people for Christ, we must meet people to tell them about Christ and invite them to come join the Trinity family. This year leaders are meeting each month in a great effort to do unprecedented outreach to the unchurched and the lost and downtrodden in the Fort Valley Area. All of our programs this year will be approached with the purpose of outreach and have the same "outreach" attached to them to remind us of what God has called the church to do. Acts 1:8 KJV says, "And ye shall receive power after the Holy Ghost has come upon you and ye shall be my witnesses."

We are also endeavoring to see our building fund grow through sacrificial giving above our tithes. We have come a long way from our start last year. At present, we are near $140,000 and hope to reach our $200,000 goal this year. It has been well established that improving infrastructure allows a church to better serve its members and the community. Please join in as we endeavor to "Build a Bigger Boat to Bring in a Bigger Catch for Christ."

These goals can only be accomplished by faith. We must believe today what we are asking God to do tomorrow. Indeed, 2 Cor. 5:17 KJV says, "We walk by faith, not by sight." We must also pray. Nothing great was done in the Bible without God's people first covering their desires in prayer. James 5:16 KJV says, "The effectual, fervent prayer of the righteous availeth much."

Time is winding up. Let us work with all diligence and use our time wisely for Christ. Let's make this year the greatest year of outreach and discipleship Trinity has ever known. With God, we can do it!

Chapter 20

TRINITY'S 102ND CHURCH ANNIVERSARY

January 2014

Pastor's Pen

Praise to God for the church He established by the blood of Jesus Christ. Praise God for Trinity Baptist family and the souls that have been saved by the ministry here for 102 years. Praise God for the fellowship of spirit-filled believers at Trinity who encourage one another and fill each other's need for friendship. Praise God for the many times we have received spiritual rejuvenation from Sunday worship and Bible study at church. Praise God for the gifts of the Holy Spirit he uses to bless us through those whom he has gifted in the church. God has placed all these blessings in the church for our spiritual well-being. Therefore, let us give God praise always for the church.

Our theme this year is "Teaching Others What We have Learned" (2 Timothy 2:2 KJV). Let us endeavor to encourage participation in Christian mentoring and discipleship in 2014. We plan to offer a workshop on discipleship and mentoring to equip Trinity's members with the understanding of what successful mentoring involves. Many people who come to church are seeking guidance; we need to let them know we are available and willing to guide them in the ways of God's Word. We plan to make a special effort to increase Sunday school attendance for our youth so they may come to know the ways of Christ. We plan to engage in other forms of outreach as the Holy Spirit moves us.

Trinity family, we must always be mindful of how critical it is for us to be a constant source of encouragement for those suffering all around us in our community. We must always conduct ourselves in a godly way so that others may hear of the loving fellowship at Trinity and be drawn to come and receive encouragement from our spirits to theirs. We must strive to be a beacon of hope to all who pass by our sanctuary by our steadfast proclamation of the hope that is in Christ. Let us make our surrounding community neighbors glad that Trinity is in their midst, and when they come and fellowship with us, let's send them back to the community with a sweeter spirit than when they came in.

The work of the gospel ministry foremost exists in our hearts, hands, feet, tongues, and is financed by our wallets. The salvation of souls is our number one goal, and discipling new believers is right next to it. May every member also continue to advance their spiritual growth even as we help others take their first steps in their walk with Christ.

The greatest church member is the one who is the greatest servant. The greatest church is the church that does the greatest service. God is not necessarily looking for a big church, but he is always looking for the greatest church. Let all Trinity members resolve to serve in such a way that we become a great church for Christ! Happy 102nd anniversary!

Chapter 21

TRINITY'S 103RD CHURCH ANNIVERSARY

January 2015

Pastor's Pen

Our theme for our 103rd church anniversary is "Building the Church on the Rock of Christ." It is based upon the unwavering belief when Peter said that Jesus is the Messiah who has come to save us from our sins. If Trinity also embraces this same belief, then we are obligated to do all we can to spread the good news of salvation in Christ.

As a missionary army for Christ, the church is charged to fight against all obstacles, both material and spiritual, in order to win and strengthen souls for Christ. We must tirelessly be committed to both spiritual and numerical growth not for our own satisfaction but for the sole purpose that the kingdom of God may increase here on Earth. This commitment includes impacting both our local community and foreign lands with the love and salvation message of Jesus Christ. This is what it means to build the church on the rock of Christ.

After over eleven years of praying, giving, meeting, and planning, all indications are that we will finally be able to begin construction on a new sanctuary within the next month or two. These are exciting times, and they very well should be, given all that has gone into bringing us to this monumental point in the history of Trinity. Let us prepare to rejoice and celebrate the entire process. It is God's blessing to us for committing faithfully and sacrificially to see the vision come to fruition. We are "Building a Bigger Boat to Bring in a Bigger Catch for Christ."

Please continue to give your tithes, offerings, and sacrificial gifts as you have established a habit of doing for some time. After the sanctuary is completed, the next immediate phase is to renovate our existing structure after we move worship into the new sanctuary, God be willing. A new kitchen, larger classrooms and meeting rooms are needs the Lord has laid on my heart to share with the Trinity family.

Another longer-term goal in the future would be the construction of a gymnasium that we can use to reach local young boys and girls through recreational evangelism in basketball camps and leagues for youth. We have to do something to effect an exponential increase in outreach to the youths in our community. So many families are broken and struggling, and the children suffer the most. Introducing community youth to Christ and Christian mentors will rescue the lives of a number of them. The completion of the sanctuary will only mark one phase of our efforts and plans to expand. I pray that Trinity will be a church family who values outreach and continues to invest in it.

I want to thank all of our seasoned saints who continue in their faithful services at Trinity after already giving decades of tireless work for the Lord. We would not be where we are today if it had not been for your sacrificial dedication. I especially want to give thanks to a number of our younger members who have taken it upon themselves to serve in leadership positions. It encourages all church members to see that Trinity is passing on the baton of faith and that our future is in the hands of young believers who are committed to sharing the love of Christ.

When all is said and done, only what we do for Christ will last. Let's make a commitment that everything we do will be for the honor of Christ and that our labor will draw multitudes closer to him. This is a guaranteed winning strategy for the church because it was Christ who said, "If I be lifted up from the Earth, I'll draw all men unto me" (John 12:32 KJV).

Happy 103rd anniversary, Trinity family! Until Christ returns …

Chapter 22

TRINITY'S 104TH CHURCH ANNIVERSARY

January 2016

Pastor's Pen

Thanks be to God, we have had our groundbreaking ceremony and construction is slated to begin on the new sanctuary in the next few weeks. After thirteen years of saving, praying, meeting, and planning, all systems are "go" for construction to start. There is a lot of anxiousness, excitement, and even some anxiety in the air, but we press on to do a great work for the Lord and for future generations of Trinity members. Renfroe Construction Company has set a timeline of ten months to completion; therefore, it is possible that we will be celebrating Christmas in the new sanctuary. We are not there yet, but we certainly can say we have already begun the journey.

The architectural rendering we've seen reveals a beautiful sanctuary that will be a sight to see. However, we must be mindful that we are not constructing a museum but rather a hospital for the sick and the lost, a house of fellowship for all in the community, a place of refuge for those beaten and battered by trials of life, a place of solace for those in mourning, and most of all, a place of salvation for those who are lost in sin. Yes, this sanctuary will be much, much more than bricks and mortar. While it is a physical edifice, it is dedicated to and designed to make an impact in the spiritual world for Christ.

What excites me just as much and maybe more so than a new sanctuary is the new

113

uses it will open up for the present sanctuary and fellowship hall. The present sanctuary will become a spacious fellowship hall and multipurpose space that will be used for children's church and can be made available for community meetings and ceremonies to draw people to the church. The fellowship hall will become a great space for ministry tailored to children four to six years of age. With a new nursery being constructed in the new sanctuary, serving babies from infancy to three years, we will have a facility that has a space designated to serving every age. We will be equipped to serve every member of the family. We want to be a family church, and now we have the opportunity to minister to all family members on a larger level.

All of this is slated to begin right after our 104th church anniversary. This year's celebration will no doubt be about looking forward more than remembering the past. Thank you to all Trinity members who not only share the vision for our future but also whose continued faithfulness, prayers, commitments, and sacrificial giving of the past and present that have brought us this far. As some deacons have been known to pray, and we also say, "Let's run on and see what the end is going to be." Happy 104th anniversary! To God be the glory, honor, and praise!

APPENDIX

Historical Highlights

Established: Trinity Baptist Church, January, 1912
Founders: Thirty-five individuals from Shiloh Baptist Church, Fort Valley, Georgia
First pastor: Reverend Cyrus S. Wilkins
First services: Mutual Aid Benefit Hall, corner of Spruce and Pine Street, Fort Valley
Property purchased on present site, April 11, 1914
Construction began under Reverend S. M. Hawkins, third pastor

1929

Church building completed by Reverend J. L. Walker
First cornerstone service, October 6
Liquidated debt of $900
Two classrooms annexed to church
Funds for annex donated by the Southern Baptist Convention's Home Mission
First church clerk: Vashi Walden

1940s

Host church: third annual Baptist youth conference for Baptist Negro students in Georgia, February 26–28, 1943

1950s

Vigilante Club organized, September 1952

1960s

Renovation of sanctuary (furniture, pews, and so forth), 1961
Restrooms added in vestibule, 1963
Property purchased, 1966, 1968
W. S. M. Banks, first black candidate to qualify for a public office in Fort Valley
J. C. Simmons, first black to serve on Peach County Hospital Authority Board, Fort Valley
Houston Stallworth, founder, Citizenship Education Commission, 1964

1970s

Civil right protestors held rally at Trinity
Civil rights marchers (white and black) spent night at Trinity
C. J. Edwards challenges Georgia's disenfranchisement law
C. J. Edwards, first black elected to serve in the city government in Fort Valley
Groundbreaking for Anderson /Walker Annex, 1972
Anderson/Walker Annex completed, 1973
Rededication service for church renovation, March 28, 1976
First marquee built, 1976
First Boy Scout Troop 245 sponsored by Trinity
Honorable Shirley Chisholm, US congressional representative, Twelfth Congressional District, spoke at Trinity during a political rally, 1976
J. C. Simmons invited to serve as chaplain at the Georgia House of Representatives, Atlanta, Georgia, March 2, 1979

1980s

Prayer bench donated by Deacon and Mrs. William Arnold
Memorial commemorative nameplates added to pews, 1981
Mortgage burned, November 1981
Second Cornerstone ceremony, June 20, 1982
Church damaged by storm, 1982
Host church, Congress of Christian Education, 1982
Returned to new sanctuary, March 18, 1984
Rededication service for new sanctuary, June 10–17, 1984
Bernice Eaton, first archivist appointed by Reverend Simmons

1990s

Trinity's church van purchased, 1994
Property purchased adjacent to the church, 1998
Dorcas opened food bank, 1998
Alley north of the church deeded to Trinity, 1999
Trinity's church history included in city of Fort Valley time capsule, 1999

2000s

Church steeple added, 2001
Website developed (trinitybaptistchfortvalley.org)
New marquee built to house the original bell removed from the bell tower, 2001
First Men's Retreat, 2001
Julius C. Simmons Gospel Choir organized, 2001
Bible Study, noonday and evening, initiated by Gregory E. Moore, pastor, 2001
Prayer teams organized, 2001
First new membership orientation class, 2001
Property (blockhouse) purchased, 2001

Property located on State University Drive donated anonymously, 2007
Becham property (service station and barbershop) purchased, 2007
First Women's Retreat, Dahlonega, Georgia
First Youth Retreat, St. Simons Island, Georgia
Christian Growth 101 class taught by Mary Yarber and Delia Taylor
Undeveloped street (alley) property purchased, 2011
Church bus purchased
PA system installed, 2001
Office hours established
Trinity expands with new sanctuary, 2016

Church Membership

1912–2016

Abrams, Jessica
Abrams, Linda
Retired educator, FVSU
Children:
    Gena
    Torrence
    Jessica
Grandchild: Schenericka
Adams, Tremaine
Aiken, Saturn
Allen, Jerry A.
Allen, Laqueta
Allen, Lee Clara (d. 1977)
Husband: Daniel
Children:
    Daniel Jr.
    Louise
    Margaret
    Nettie
    Lucille
Amica, Jaylen
Anderson, Benjamin S., Sr.
(1904–1971)
Retired educator, FVSC
Wife: Lula Mae Sutton
Anderson, Idella M. (1893–1971)
Children:
    Wilma Jean
Anderson, Leroy
Wife: Sandra

Anderson, Lula Mae Sutton
(1907–1955)
Husband: Benjamin S.
Children:
Benjamin, Jr.
Anderson Robert
Wife: Rosa
Anderson, Rosa
Husband: Robert
Anderson, Sandra
Husband: Leroy
Grandchild:
    Zion Rouse
Anderson, Wilma Jean (1919–1989)
Retired educator, FVSC
Appling, Ann
Appling, Oliver (1935–2014)
Joined 1989
Armstrong, Reverend and Mrs.
Armstrong, Tom
Armstrong, Annie Lou Canady
    (See also Gray)
Armstrong, Minister Eddie
Wife: Sheryl
Armstrong, Sheryl
Husband: Minister Eddie
Arnold, Angeola Jackson (1912–2004)
Retired educator, Peach County school
system
Husband: William
Children:
    Martin, Barbara Ann
    Arnold, Casey J.

Arnold, Casey J.

Arnold, Everett

Arnold, William E. (1916–2002)

Retired, FVSC

Wife: Angeola Jackson

Arrant, A.

Retired: Postal Service

Arrant, Maeleen

Jeanes Supervisor

Avent, Hattie C. (d. 1978)

Baker, Essie

Baldwin, Garrette

Baldwin, Mattie Mathis (d. 1968)

Baldwin, Ransom (d. 2015)

Baldwin, Thelma

Banks, Hattie

Retired educator, Peach County school system

Husband: W. S. M. Banks

Children:

    W. S. M. Banks, Jr.

Banks, Kevin

Banks, William S. M. (1915–2007)

Retired educator and administrator, FVSC

Wife: Hattie

Barner, Marilyn

Barrett, Annie Ruth King

Barrett-Huff, Jenita Joann

Beauford, Evelyn

Husband: Samuel

Children:

    Yvonne

    Cynthia

    Samuel, Jr.

    Harriet

Beauford, Samuel (d. 1984)

Wife: Evelyn

Beauford, Yvonne

See Oliver

Beck, Dajeria

Beck, Jakeria

Bellamy, Donna Denise

Children:

    Benita Scott

Bellamy, Donnita D.

Bellamy, Juanita

Retired educator, Peach County school system

Husband: Donnie

Children:

    Donna D.

    Donnita D.

Grandchildren:

    Benita Scott

Bennet, Velma

Belt, William

Bingham, Percella

Children:

    Yvette

Bingham, RaShawn

Bingham, Yvette

Blount, Leola C. (1924–1993)

Husband: Malcolm

Children:

    Carmen

    Daryl

    Juanita

    Lita

    Malcolm Jr.

Blount, Malcolm (1920–1988)
Retired educator, FVSC
Wife: Leola C.
Blue, Lorene
Bogan, Reginald
Bowden, LaQuinta
Boyer, Antoine
Boyer, Faye
Children:
    Lauryn E.
Boyer, Jeanette
Boyer, Wayne E.
Children:
    Antoine
Brewton, Inez
Retired educator, Houston County
school system
Husband: Philip
    Phyllis
    Kristy LaVee,
Brewton, Philip
Retired educator
Wife: Inez
Brinson, Elizabeth
Retired educator, FVSC
Children:
    Susan
    Patricia
    Jimmy
    Kenneth
    Lenard
Brinson, Susan
Broadnax, Anthony
Brooks, Margaret
Brown, Carol

Children:
    Kira
    Ashley
    Breona
Brown, Corine (1903–1979)
Brown, Derek Lamar
Brown, Dontrell
Brown, Early (d. 1976)
Brown, Evelyn
    (See McCoy)
Brown, Jakeisha M.
Brown, Kira
Brown, Lillian
Brown, Lucile
Brown, Marquez
Brown, Mary
Brown, Maude
Brown, Robert
Brown, Sabrina
Children:
    Marzuez
    Shanequa
    Devonta
Brown, Samuel
Brown, Willie (d. 1993)
Wife: Lucile
Bryant, Ellen
Bryant, Joe
Bryant, Will
Bryant, Willie J.
Buckner, Vera
Burden, Celestine Johnson
Children:
    Lamaud
    Larry

Burden, Lamaud
Burden, Larry
Burton-Junior, Eva
    (See also Junior)
Children:
    Leslie Monique
    Lori Michelle
Burse, Mamie
First Lady, FVSU
Husband: Luther
Children:
    Elizabeth
    Luther, Jr.
Burse, Dr. Luther
FVSU president
Wife: Mamie
Butler, David
Butts, Jessica
Byrd, Nettie
Caldwell, Counsel
Calhoun, Lula G.
Canady, Annie Lou
    (See also Armstrong)
Canady, Charlie
Canady, Clara
Husband: Clark
Children:
    Charlie
    Wallace
    Annie Lou
    Obie
    Ailean
    Alice
Canady, Clark
Wife: Clara

Canady, Daisy Lingo (1910–1985)
Husband: Wallace
Children:
    Marie
    Pauline
Canady, Reverend Henry
Canady, Irene
Canady, Marie
    (See Cleveland and Taylor)
Canady, Wallace (d. 1980)
Retired Contractor and Tree Pruner
Wife: Daisy
Canady, Wylean
Carter, Justin
Carter, Lydia Rocanne
Carter, Tierra
Carthon, Annie Releford (1944–1995)
FVSU professor
Children:
    Brandley Curtis
    Shawn
Chamblis, Narissa
Chatman, Christie B.
Chatman, Elanne
Chellers, Gussie
Childs, Jeffrey E.
Church, Robert Thomas (1909–2009)
Retired: Agricultural Extension County
Agent in Peach County
Wife: Ruby
Children:
    Anita
    Robert, Jr.
Clark, Annie Ruth
Husband: Dennis

Children:
    Blanche C. Atkinson
Clark, Dennis
Wife: Annie Ruth
Cleveland, Marie C. (1928–2002)
Retired Educator: Taylor County
school system
Coleman, Joanne
Coleman, Sheilee
Colvard, Bridget
    (See Miller)
Conteh, Alfred, Sr.
Children:
    Alfred, Jr.
    Alvin
Conteh, Dorothy Burns
Retired educator and administrator,
FVSU
Children:
    Jolita Burns
    Alfred
    Alvin
Corker, Ernest
Retired Veterinarian
Wife: Grace
Corker, Grace
Retired educator and businessperson
Husband: Ernest
Children:
    Gregory
    Cynthia
Cornelius, David (d. 1980)
Retired, Crawford County school sys-
tem and businessman
Wife: Madie

Cornelius, Geraldine S.
Cornelius, Madie (d. 2015)
Retired businessperson
Husband: David
Children:
    Frederick
    Denise
    Vendya
    Dwight
Cox, Cedric
Crim, Jazmin
Crumbly, Dorothy
Retired administrator, FVSU
Husband: Isaac
Children:
Isaac Ooyiman
Konata Ato
Crumbly, Isaac
Wife: Dorothy
Cruver, Neris
Daniely, Barbara
Retired educator, Peach County school
system
Husband: Clarence
Children:
    Andrena
Daniely, Clarence
Retired educator,
Wife: Barbara
Daniely, Clyde
Daniely, Larry (1950–1994)
Educator, Bibb County school system
Daniels, Ada W.
Dantly, L. C.
Dassau, Ronald

Davis, Alice
Husband: John
Children:
    Johnny
    (See also Ross)
Davis, Carolyn
Davis, Ernest
Davis, Estella
Davis, Evelyn
    (See McCray)
Davis, Johnnie C.
Davis, Lamashia
Davis, Lura Frances
Davis, Lessie
    (See also Felder)
Davis, Mary Bell Ragin
Davis, Willie B. (1918–1987)
Dawson, Anna
Dawson, Edward (Ed)
Dean, Charlie Mae
Dean, Clemont
Dean, Loistine Morgan Smith
    (See also Smith)
Demons, Jacquelyn Yvonne Smith
(1938–2009)
Husband: John
Children:
    Jamehl
Demons, John
Wife: Jacquelyn
Dent, Annie
Derico, Aggie
Devoe, Paris
Dickerson, Cheryl
Dorsey, Vivian

Drain, Carolyn
Dubart, Lila
Duffie, Mack
Wife: Ruby
Duffie, Ruby
Husband: Mack
Grandchildren:
    Justin Carter
    Hosea Carter
Dugger, Iyunci
Dunlap, Florence Mae McCrary
(1943–2007)
Retired, Peach County Hospital
Durham, Katherine
Dyson, Barbara
Husband: Marvin
Children:
    Marvin, Jr.
    Felice
    Tangie Yvette
    Tracey Lorraine (1969–1975)
Dyson, Edward
Dyson, Marvin
Wife: Barbara
Eaton, Bernice
Retired educator, FVSU
Husband: David
Children:
    David M. II
    Deidre
    Darryl
Eaton, David (1928–2008)
Retired educator, FVSU
Wife: Bernice
Edwards, Alfred Jerome (1954–1994)

Assistant director, Edwards Funeral
Home
Edwards, Andrew J. Jr.
Wife:
Edwards, Andrew Jackson, Sr.
(1921–1972)
Wife: Zodie
Edwards, Arita
Edwards, Betty
Edwards, Claybon (1929–2015)
Director, C. J. Edwards Funeral Home
Wife: Mary
Edwards, Julia
    (1975)
Husband: Martin
Children:
    Andrew J. (AJ)
    Claybon J.
    Mary J.
    Eloise
    Mildred
    Hazel
Edwards, Martin (1900–1988)
    First wife: Julia
    Second wife: Rilla King
Edwards, Mary
Husband: Claybon
Children:
    Denise
Edwards, Mary Julia
    (See Marshall)
Edwards, Rilla King (1921–1988)
Husband: Martin Edwards
    (See also King)
Edwards, Zodie (1920–1998)

Husband: Andrew (AJ)
Children:
    Diane
    Cassandria
    Andrew
    Alfred
    Arita
Ellison, Penny
Emanuel, Annie Lee
Emanuel, Alberta
Emanuel, Bertha
Husband: Carl
Children:
    Annie Lee
    Rosa Lee
Emanuel, Carl
Wife: Bertha
Emanuel, Rosa Lee
Etta, Victor
Evans, Patricia
Evans, Retha
Evans, Rosa Lee
Evans, Rosa M.
Everett, Desmond
Ezell, Yancey Thaddeus
Farkas, Patricia
Favors, Janie (d. 1980)
Retired nurse
Felder, Beulah
Felder, Dye
Wife: Lelia
Felder, Mr. and Mrs. Julius
Children:
    Lillie B.
Felder, Laura

Felder, Lelia
Husband: Dye
Children:
    Lessie
    Susie
Felder, Lillie B.
    (See also Miller)
Felder, Susie
    (See Davis)
Felton, Barbara Ann Martin
(1952–1992)
Children:
    Casey
Felton, Corine Clark
Floyd, Hattie (See Wilson)
    (See also Wynn)
Fluellen, Florence Robinson (d. 1995)
Fluellen, Meaza
Fluellen, Willie Florence
Ford, Cedric
Ford, Louis
Ford, Sallie
Ford, Samuel
Ford, Walter T. (d. 1946)
Ford, Willie
Foster, Willie E.
Frazier, Fred
Freeman, Cumesha
Freeman, Stephanie Childs
Children:
    Jaylon Amica
Fuller, Annie
Husband: John
Fuller, John
Wife: Annie

Fuller, Lula
Fuller, Robert
Gadsden, Ada M.
Garrard, Reginald
Gause, Valshea Lucy
Gibson, Angela
Gibson, Arthur
Gibson, Darion
Giles, Hope
Husband: Leonard
Children:
    Arnold
    Melissa Faith
Giles, Leonard
Wife: Hope
Glover, Calvin Keith
Goodwin, A.
Goolsby, Leroy
Gore, Lawanda K. (1968–2015)
Gray, Annie Lou Canady (1889–1965)
Husband: Jacee
    (See also Armstrong)
Children:
    Annie Florence
Green, Earnestine
Green, Frank
Green, Jamarcus
Green, Julissa
Green, Larry
Hand, Bernice
Retired: Warner Robins Air Force
Elementary school system
Husband: Sidney Taylor
Children:
    Beverly

Sidney, T. Jr.
Hand, Sidney Taylor (1930–2011)
Wife: Bernice
Harden, Mike
Harley, Shytina
Harris, Dontrell
Harris, George Edward, Jr.
(1943–1997)
Harris, Gloria Jean Bryant Street
    (See also Street)
Retired Educator, Bibb County school
system
Husband: Willie
Harris, Irene F. Moore
Harris, Lillie Mae
Harris, Mary
Harris, Shelva
Haslam, Marilyn C.
Hawkins, Chauncil Talton
Hawkins, Elizabeth Victoria Hamilton
(1915–2006)
Retired educator, Peach County school
system
Husband: Coach James E. Hawkins
Children:
    David Butler
Hayes, Mary
Henderson, Lillian
Henry, David
Henton, Antonio
Wife: Royalle
Henton, Cosey
Henton, Royalle
Husband: Antonio
Hicks, Murlenum (1912–1993)

Husband: Odess E.
Children:
    Marian
    Carolyn
Hicks, Odess E. (d. 1978)
Wife: Marlenum
Hiley, Andrea
Hiley, Irene
Hodges, Rochelle
    (See also Pearson)
Hogan, Andrea
Hogan, Anita McCray
    (See also McCray)
Husband: Richard Thomas
Children:
    Richard II
    Timothy
    Jonathan
Hogan, Jonathan
Hogan, Richard II
Children:
    Jackson
    Jalen
    Jordan
Hogan, Richard Thomas
Wife: Anita
Hogan, Timothy
Hollinshed, Alice
Hollinshed, Annie R. (1925–1949)
Hollinshed, Daisy
Hollinshed, Dorothy
Hollinshed, Ellenor
Hollinshed, Gloria
Hollinshed, Hennie Robinson
Hollinshed, Jewel

Hollinshed, Leon
Hollinshed, Mae Alice
Hollinshed, Margaret
Hollinshed, Mary Alice
Hollinshed, Patience
Hooten, Robert Lee
Hope, Winfred
Horton, Alre G.
Wife: Tisa Talton
Horton, Cornelius
Wife: Dollie
Horton, Dollie
Husband: Cornelius
Children:
    Alrae
    Roderick (Rod)
Horton, Tisa Lotia Talton
Children:
    Alisa
    Talton, Nigel
Houston, L. H.
Howard, Frank
Huff, Jeanette King
    (See also King)
Husband: McDonnell
Children:
    Jenita Joan Barrett
Huggins, Carl
Huggins, Getter (d. 1996)
Wife: Mary
Huggins, Mary (1939–2013)
Husband: Getter
Children:
    Sharon
    Kirk

    Carl
Hunt, LaShauna Jackson
Husband: Randall
Children:
    Hannah
    Sa'Riah
    Gabriel Hunt
Hunt, Miriam T.
Hunt, Randall
Wife: LaShauna
Hunter, Harold
Hunter, James
Hutchenson, Frank
Hutchenson, Mrs. Frank
Ingram, Eric
Isom, James
Isom, Rosa (1965)
Jackson, Angeola
    (See Arnold)
Jackson, Beauford Lee (1910–1993)
Jackson, Clita
Jackson, Elizabeth
Jackson, Ethel
    (See Stamps)
Jackson, Ken
Jackson, Lewis
Jackson, Lonnie
Jackson, Magnolia
Jackson, Minnie
Jackson, Namia Smith
Jackson, Nancy Elizabeth (1975)
Jackson, Rena
Jackson, Veronica
Jackson, Wilmetta
    (See Smith)

(See also Langston)
(See also McSee)
Jacob, Lila
Jenkins, Joyce (d.2016)
Jennings, Mary
Jessie, Irene Smith
Johnson, Alberta
    (See Rumph)
Johnson, Annie S.
Johnson, Celestine
    (See Burden)
Johnson, Diane
    (See Meadows)
Johnson, Eddie S.
Johnson, Ernest
Johnson, Irene
Johnson, James
Johnson, Jared
Johnson, Jarrett C.
Johnson, Leroy
Johnson, Lewis (d.2004)
Children:
    Curtis
Johnson, Louise
Johnson, Obie
Johnson, Odell Robinson
Johnson, Susie
    (See also Felder)
Jones, Avon F.
Jones, Betty
Husband: Calanda
Children:
    Venetta
Jones, Calanda
Wife: Betty

Jones, George
Wife: Rosa
Jones, Jessica
Jones, Leon
Jones, Mrs. Leon
Jones, Katinell
Jones, Mary
Jones, Monaye
Jones, Rosa
Husband: George
Jones, Ruth
Jones, Venetta
Children:
    Zaniyah
Jordan, Anna Williams
Jordan, Felicia
Jordan, Freddie M.
Children:
    Michael
    Philip
    David
    Diane
Jordan, Mattie Kate Marshall
Jordan, Michael
Jordan, Philip U.
Wife: Anna Williams
Children:
    Aidasia Moore
Jordan, Richard
Jowers, George, Jr. (1924–1984)
Joyner, Helen
Husband: Henry W.
Children:
    Sandra
    Eloise

Gordan
Joyner, Henry W.
Wife: Helen
Junior, Eva Burton
Husband: Ester James, Jr.
Children:
 Leslie M. Burton
 Lori M. Burton
Junior, Ester James Jr.
Wife: Eva Burton
Kendrick, Charlotte
Kendrick, Katina W.
Children:
 Eric Taylor
 Kynadi A.
Kenney, Kareem D.
Wife: Kristy B.
Kenney, Kristy
Husband: Kareem D.
 (See also Brewton)
Children:
 Kaylen
Kimbro, Lillian
Husband: Obie
Kimbro, Obie
Wife: Lillian
King, Rilla
Husband: Reverend King
 (See also: Edwards)
Children:
 Joan
 Jeanette
 Annie Ruth
 Donnis
King, Tonya D.

Kinnel, Mary
Knighton, Markease
Knolton, Darran
Langston, Charles Sr.
Wife: Wilmetta
Langston, Wilmetta S.
Retired, Houston County school
system
 (See also: Smith)
 See Jackson)
 (See McSee)
Children:
 Charles (Chuck) Jr.
Lawrence, Gerald Jr.
Lavender, Doris D. (1929–1999)
Husband: Tendrill H.
Children:
 Philip
 Anita
Lavender, Tendrill H.
Wife: Doris
Lawrence, Gerald Jr.
Leary, Deontate
Lee, Corinthia
Lee, Margaret
Lewis, Daisy L (1913–2001)
Children:
 Robert
Lewis, Rashon
Lindsey, Walter
Lindsey, Ozzie Daniely
Children:
 Walter
Little, Julia Wynn
 (See also Wynn)

Gail

Jacqueline

Paulette

Avis

Anita

McCray, Lucrista

McCullough, William

McGhee, Mary

McGhee, Viola (1978)

Children:

Ella

McIntyre, Beulah F.

McLendon, Mattie

Macomson, Elizabeth

Husband: William

Macomson, William

Wife: Elizabeth

McRae, Ernest

Wife: Lorene

McRae, Lorene C.

Husband: Ernest

Children:

Ernest

Michelle

McSee, Wilmetta

(See Langston)

Maddox, Elizabeth

Maddox, Ida Bell (1891–1987)

Madison, Cynthia

Maeod, Destiny

Magee, Audrey

Husband: Charles

Children:

Candice Nicole

Darian

Magee, Charles

Wife: Audrey

Mangram, Pricilla

Husband: Coach Mangram

Children:

Kimberly

Perry

Mann, Montana

Manuel, Oliver

Wife: Ella

Marable, John

Marshall, Bertha (1963)

Marshall, Karen

Marshall, Mary Julia

Children:

Karen

Marshall, Stanley

Martin, Barbara Ann

(See Arnold)

Martin, Lajuan

Martin, Lecrecia

Martin, M. Mernelle

Mathis, Alice Mae (1913–2012)

Children:

Edward Moody

JD

Walter Ben

Carl

Melvyn

Mildred

Eloise

Charlie Lynn

Bettye

Marvin

Mathis, Jewell Daniely

Children:
    Walter
    Opie
    Roni
Mathis, Lula Howard (1869–1966)
Mathis, Mary
Children:
    Ricky
Mathis, Mrs. William S.
Mathis, Opie
Mathis, Roni
Mathis, Walter B. Jr.
Mathis, Wynette
Children:
    Richard III
    (See Smith)
Maxwell, Janessa
Meadows, Derrick
Meadows, Dianne Jordan
    (See also Jordan)
Children:
    Adderika
Meeks, Victoria
Miller, Bobbie G.
Miller, Bridgett Colvard
Husband: Minister Douglas
Miller, Carrie
Miller, Connie
Miller, Minister Douglas
Wife: Bridgett Colvard
Miller, Gladys
Miller, Lillie B. Felder
Miller, Mary (1882–1973)
Miller, Nathaniel
Miller, Debarriaus

Mitchell, Alfred
Wife: Mattie
Mitchell, Mattie
Husband: Alfred
Children:
    Will
Moody, Alberta Holmes (1914–2012)
Retired educator, Houston County
public school system
Husband: John
Children:
    Ronnie G.
Moody, John (d. 2000)
Retired
Wife: Alberta
Moody, Ronnie G. Sr.
Wife: Talisha C.
Moody, Talisha Carter
Husband: Ronnie
Children:
    Ronnie G. Jr.
    Seth
Moore, Aidasia
Moore, Edward
Moore, Reverend Dr. Gregory E.,
pastor, Trinity Missionary Baptist
Church
Wife: Dr. Helen-Louise, MD
Moore, Dr. Helen-Louise
Husband: Reverend Dr. Gregory E.
Children:
    William G.
    Mary Grace
    Christianna

Moorehead, William D. Sr.
(1929–2014)
Retired educator and administrator,
FVSU
Wife: Willie D. White
Moorehead, William Douglas Jr.
Moorehead, Willie D. W.
Retired Peach County public school
system
Husband: William D. Sr.
Children:
    Wynette
    William Douglas, Jr.
    Yvette
    Lynette
Morgan, Dave
Morgan, Duncan (d. 1989)
Morgan, James
Morgan, Kelvin Lamar
Morgan, Loistine
    (See Dean)
    (See Smith)
Morgan, Martha
    (See Simmons)
Morgan, Mary
Morgan, Maude Thomas
Husband: Dave
Children:
    Louisteen
    Martha
Morgan, Sheila Denise
Moss, Sonja Y.
Murphy, Carrie Young (1922–1996)
Retired, Peach County public school
system

Husband: Vincent
Children:
    Vincent, Jr.
    Llewellyn
    Melvin
Murphy, Vincent Sr. (1919–1989)
Wife: Carrie
Myers, Karen
Children:
    Pearson, Justin
Myers, Kelly R.
Nelson, Addie
Children:
    Cheryl
    Cynara
Nelson, Cheryl
Nelson, Cynara
Nelson, Shannon
Children:
    Mariena
Nesmith, Ashlee
Nix, Fannie Williams
Teacher
Husband: Henry
Children:
    Lillian
    Fannie
Nix, Henry
Wife: Fannie Williams
Nix, Shirley
Nobles, Mick'aela
Obeng, Eric
O'Bryant, Albert
Wife: Deliah
Osofu-Anim, George

Oliver, Yvonne Beauford
Retired educator and administrator, FVSU
    (See also Beauford)
Palmer, Barbara H.
Retired educator, FVSU
Husband: Thomas
Children:
    Tomia Esperanza
    Felica
    Corey
Palmer, Thomas
Retired administrator, FVSU
Wife: Barbara H.
Pearson, Ozias
Wife: Shirley
Pearson, Rochelle
Pearson, Shirley
Husband: Ozias
Pepper, Ashley
Perry, Jeanette
Pitts, Wilbur
Plant, Justin
Plant, Lewanna
    Justin
    Shavodus
    (See Streeter)
Plant, Shavodus
Plant, Shanequa L.
Ponder, Clifford Nellion (1936–1913)
Retired educator and administrator, FVSU
Wife: Margie
Ponder, Margie J.
Retired FVSU Administrator

Husband: Clifford Nellion
Children:
    Anita Jeanettte
    Keisha Estelle
    Celesete Alexander
Poole, Izeola
Husband: Travern (Tre)
Poole, Travern (Tre)
Wife: Izeola
Porter, Annie Mae Canady (1910–1991)
Children:
    Malone
    Cecil
    Clifford
Postell, Devonta
Postell, Dontae
Postell, Willie M.
Prater, Jacqueline (d. 1998)
First Lady, FVSU
Prater, Oscar L.
FVSU president
Price, Maude
Pugh, Geneva
Ragin, Keith Calvin
Reed, John
Wife: Joyce
Previous church: Emanuel Baptist Church, Elmont, NY
Reed, Joyce
Husband: John
Rice, Ida Mae
Richard, Rosa Bell Young (d. 1977)
    (See Young)

Ricks, Gwendolyn

Roberson, Arthur
Wife: Ofhieldia B.
Roberson, Florence (1930–2000)
Roberson, Ofhieldia B. (1900–1988)
Husband: Arthur
Children:
  Cleo
  Florence
  Arthur, Jr.
Robinson, Annie M.B.
(1929–1994)
Robinson, Talania
Ross, Alice Davis (1900–2003)
Husband: Henry
  (See Davis)
Ross, Katie Murphy (d. 1972)
Ross, Mattie
Ross, Niki
Ross, Ruth
Rouse, Edith
Children:
  Jakeisha Thomas
  Jaylon Thomas
  Tremaine Adams
  Darran Knolton
Grandchild:
  Zion Rouse
Rouse, Louise Hollinshed (1910–1987)
Husband: Henry
Rumph, Alberta Johnson (1909–2000)
Husband: Willie
Rumph, Nettie
Sampson, Gladyce Carter (d. 1983)
FVSC educator

Sanders, Helen Louise Young
(1911–1997)
  (See also Young)
Husband: Chester
Satchell, Mary (1893–1982)
Husband: Elbert
Scippio, R. L.
Scott, Benita Shaw
Settle, Terrence
Simmons, Alma Alexander
(1927–2012)
Retired educator, FVSU
Husband: Reverend Julius Caesar
Simmons Sr.
Children:
  Patricia Diane
  Julius C.
  Paron
Simmons, Clarence (1935–1988)
Simmons, Cleo
Simmons, Gertis Williams
Simmons, Reverend Julius Caesar Sr.
(1999)
Retired FVSU administrator
Pastor, Trinity Baptist Church
Wife: Alma Alexander
Simmons, Martha Maude (1922–1987)
  (See also: Morgan)
Simmons, Paron Jahmone(PJ)
Simmons, Pinkie
Sims, Motta
Singh, Faye
Children:
  Millicent
  Alya Gabrielle

Slappey, Tom
Small, Denise Edwards
    (See also Edwards)
Husband: Anthony
Children:
    Sabastain
    Samantha
    Courtney
    Caitlin
Smith, Alfred (d. 1988)
Smith, Amos
Wife: Evelyn
Smith, Beverly L.
Husband: Reverend George
Children:
    Christina
    Kyle
Smith, Charlie
Smith, Cherilyn
Smith, Cornell
Smith, Eric
Smith, Evelyn Neal Childs (d. 2004)
Retired educator, Macon County
school system
Husband: Amos
Children:
    Erica
Smith, Frank
Smith, George L.
Smith, Inez J.
Husband: Reverend William A. Sr.
Children:
    Wilmetta
    Theresa
    William, Jr.

    Martin
    John
    Henry
Smith, Jackie
Smith, Jarvis
Smith, Kyle Ellington G.
Smith, Loistine Morgan
Children:
    Louis T. Jr.
    (See also Morgan)
    (See also Dean)
Smith, Oscar James Jr. (1960–1998)
Smith, Reverend George
Wife: Beverly
Smith, Ronnie J.
Smith, Rosa B. Young
    (See also Young)
Smith, Sallie
Smith, Reverend William A. Sr.
Wife: Inez
Smith, Willie
Smith, Wilmetta
    (See Langston)
    (See also Jackson)
    (See also McSee)
Smith, Wynette
    (See also Moorehead)
    (See also Mathis)
Husband: Isaac (Ike)
Children:
    Ikeia
Stallworth, Houston (1978)
Stamps, Bessie (1947)
Children:
    Emory

Taylor, Ida
Taylor, John Jr.
Retired: Administrator FVSU
Wife: Delia
Taylor, Katina Raquel
Children:
    Taylor, Eric
    (See Kendrick)
    (See also Weatherspoon)
Taylor, Marie Cleveland
    (See also Canady)
    (See also Cleveland)
Taylor, Tuesday
Telfair, Stephanie McBurroughs
    (See McBurroughs)
Tennyson, Brenton
Tennyson, LaTondra
Thomas, Anne P. Madison (1912–1993)
Husband: John
Thomas, Floyd
Thomas, Jaylon
Thomas, John C.
(1905–1983)
Wife: Ann
Thomas, Patience
Maude Morgan
Thompson, Mary Elizabeth
Thompson, R. N.
Thornton, Helene (1937–2001)
Tolen, Jacqueline E.
Children:
    Ware, Mya
    Ware, Tyler
Toomer, Charles
Towns, Daniel (1979)

Wife: Beatrice C.
Children:
    James
    Sylvester
    Juanita
    Betty
    Martha
    Annette
    Olivia
    Patricia
    Rose Marie
Towns, Daniel (1979)
Wife: Delia
Towns, Delia
Husband: Daniel
Towns, Elia
Troup, Dr. Cornelius V. Sr.
Retired FVSC president
Wife: Katye
Troup, Katye Murphy
(1906–1984)
First Lady, FVSU
Husband: Dr. Cornelius V.
Children:
    Cornelius (Connie) V. Jr.
    Eliott V.
    Kenneth
Tucker, Marion
Turner, Beverly
    (See also Ware)
Turner, Darius
Turner, Ellen
Turner, James
Turner, Karen
    (See also Talton)

Children:

    Marquis Quintel

    Darius Bernard

    Keaya Nicolle

Turner, Mattie Ruth

(1933–2004)

Children:

    Joe

    John L.

    James

    Jeffrey

    Beverly

    Carolyn

    Robin

    Juandolyn C.

Underwood, Pearl M.

Vance, Brenda

Husband: Luther

Children:

    Victor

    Vonda

Vance: Dr. Luther Sr.

Wife: Brenda

Walden, Vashti Williams

Walker, Diane E.

Walker, Emma

Practical Nurse

Husband: Reverend John L. Walker

Walker, Jeraldine

Husband: Melvin

Children:

    Daphne

    Melvin Jr

Walker, Melvin

Wife: Jeraldine

Walker, Reverend John L.

Pastor, Trinity Baptist Church

Teacher

Wife: Emma

Ward, Carlos

Ware, Beverly Jean

    (See also Turner)

Warren, Issie

Husband: Reverend Charlie

Children:

    Alice

Warren, Lillie B.

Warren, Susie B.

Warren, Reverend Charlie

Wife: Issie

Weatherspoon, Brenda S.

Retired educator

Husband: Elijah

Children:

    Kevin Genard

    Katinia Raquel

    Kerey Elijah

Weatherspoon, Elijah

Retired coach and educator, Houston

County school system

Wife: Brenda

Weatherspoon, K. Genard

Weatherspoon, Katinia R.

    (See Kendrick)

    (See also Taylor)

Weatherspoon, Kerey E.

(1981–2017)

Weldon, Annie Katherine

Wells, Eddie

Wife: Elma J.

Wells, Elma J.
Husband: Eddie
Westbrook, Exia Shortridge
Children:
    Eva Burton Junior
White, Juliet Pappas (1914–2006)
Children:
    Willie D. W. Moorehead
Wiggins, Nettie (d. 1980)
Wilburn, Wellie S.
Wilcox, Sandra
Wilkerson, Annie Pearl Zachery
(1934–2013)
Retired educator
Husband: Chester Sr.
Children:
    Chester Jr.
    Shawn Dewayne
    Angela Ulanta
Wilkerson, Chester, Jr. (1956–1991)
Children:
    Isaiah J.
Wilkerson, Chester Sr. (1930–1987)
Retired educator
Wife: Annie Pearl Zackery
Williams, Anna
Children:
    Moore, Aidasia
Williams, Cathy
Williams, Evangeline
Children:
    Cathy
    Ronald
    Angeline
Williams, Gregory

Wife: Vender
Williams, Juillet
Williams, R. L.
Williams, Robert
Williams, Ronald
Williams, Sarah
Williams, Sharon
Williams, Teassa
Williams, Thomas B.
Williams, Vender
Husband: Gregory
Williams, Viola
Willis, Corine
Willis, Thomas
Wilson, Hattie Floyd (1912–2006)
    (See also Floyd)
    (See also Wynn)
Wilson, McKinley (d. 1980)
Wife: Marcia Vivian Ophelia
Shepperson
Wilson, Marcia Vivian Ophelia
Shepperson (1911–2001)
Retired educator
Husband: McKinley
Children:
    Barbara
    Lois
    Charles
Wolfolk, Betty
Husband: Dave
Children:
    Terrance
Wolfolk, Dave
Wife: Betty
Woodson, Chuck

Wright, Breona
Wynn, Elsie
Children:
    Hattie
Wynn, Julia
Children:
    Elsie
    Lee Clara
    Maggie
Wynn, Lee Clara
    (See Allen)
Wynn, Maggie
Yarber, Isaiah
Retired
Wife: Mary
Yarber, Mary
Retired
Husband: Isaiah

Children:
    Efrem
    Tene
Young, Arthur C. Jr (1919–1999)
Wife: Flora Mae
Children:
    Florzell
    Cora Mae
    Sarah Ann
    Robert C. III
Young, Arthur Sr.
Wife: Cora Skinner
Young, Cora Skinner
Husband: Arthur Sr.
Children:
    Helen Louise
    Nellie
    Rosa
    Arthur Jr.

Music Ministry

Adult Choir

1964

Cornelius, Madie
Hicks, Odess E.
Hicks, Murlenum
Langston, Charles
McCray, Evelyn
Marshall, Mary J.
Troup, Cornelius V.

1974

Beauford, Evelyn, president
Beauford, Samuel W.
Cornelious, Madie Ruth
Daniely, Barbara
Demons, Jacquelyn
Dunlap, Florence
Dyson, Barbara
Dyson, Marvin
Edwards, Zodie
Gadsden, Ada M., secretary/treasurer
Hicks, Murlenum B.
Lavender, Doris
Marshall, Karen
Marshall, Mary J.
Mathis, Alice
McCrary, Felma
McCray, Evelyn
Sampson, Gladyce
Simmons, Martha
Smith, Evelyn

Taylor, John
Weatherspoon, Brenda
Weatherspoon, Elijah
Willis, Dr. Bessie, Musician

Chancel Choir

1975

Beauford, Evelyn
Beauford, Samuel
Cornelious, Madie Ruth
Daniely, Barbara
Demons, Jacquelyn
Dunlap, Florence, secretary/treasurer
Dyson, Barbara
Dyson, Marvin
Edwards, Zodie
Gadsden, Ada
Kimbro, Obie
Lavender, Doris
Marshall, Karen
Marshall, Mary J.
Mathis, Alice
McCrary, Felma
McCray, Evelyn
Sampson, Gladyce
Simmons, Martha
Smith, Evelyn
Taylor, John, president
Weatherspoon, Brenda
Weatherspoon, Elijah

1976

Beauford, Evelyn
Brewton, Philip
Demons, Jacquelyn, assistant secretary
Dunlap, Florence, treasurer
Gadsden, Ada M.
Hicks, Murlenum B.
Langston, Wilmetta, secretary
Lavender, Doris
Marshall, Mary J.
Mathis, Alice
McCrary, Felma
McCray, Evelyn
Marshall, Mary J.
Mathis, Alice
Palmer, Thomas
Sampson, Gladyce, vice president
Simmons, Martha
Smith, Evelyn
Taylor, John Jr., president
Taylor, Marie Canady Cleveland
Turner, Mattie Ruth
Weatherspoon, Brenda
Weatherspoon, Elijah

1977

Beauford, Evelyn
Brewton, Philip
Cornelious, Madie R.
Demons, Jacquelyn, treasurer
Dunlap, Florence
Dyson, Barbara
Edwards, Zodie
Gadsden, Ada

Garrard, Reginald
Hicks, Mrs. Mrelenum
Jowers, George
Kimbro, Lillian
Langston, Wilmetta, secretary
Lavender, Doris, assistant secretary
Marshall, Mary J.
Mathis, Alice
McCrary, Felma
McCray, Evelyn
Palmer, Thomas, vice president
Sampson, Gladyce, president
Simmons, Martha
Smith, Evelyn
Street, Gloria
Taylor, John Jr.
Taylor, Marie
Turner, Mattie Ruth
Weatherspoon, Brenda
Weatherspoon, Elijah

1980

Brewton, Phillip
Cleveland, Marie Taylor, vice president
Daniely, Barbara
Demon, Jacquelyn
Etta, Victor, Chaplain
Gadsden, Ada M.
Hicks, Murlenum
Jowers, George, president
Kimbro, Lillian
Konan, Jackie
Langston, Wilmetta S., secretary
Lavender, Doris

Marshall, Mary Julia
Mathis, Alice
McCray, Evelyn
Moorehead, Yvette, organist
Palmer, Thomas
Sampson, Gladyce
Simmons, Martha
Street, Gloria, assistant secretary/
treasurer
Taylor, John
Turner, Mattie Ruth
Weatherspoon, Brenda, director
Weatherspoon, Elijah
Weldon, Annie Ruth
Williams, Robert

1984

Brewton, Phillip
Cleveland, Marie Taylor
Daniely, Barbara
Demons, Jacquelyn
Gadsden, Ada M., president
Jowers, George
Kimbro, Lillian
Konan, Jackie
Langston, Wilmetta S., secretary
Lavender, Doris
Magee, Audrey
Marshall, Mary Julia
Palmer, Thomas
Simmons, Martha, chaplain
Smith, Evelyn
Taylor, John
Turner, Mattie Ruth

Street, Gloria, treasurer/assistant
secretary
Stripling, Gregory, pianist
Weatherspoon, Brenda, director
Weatherspoon, Elijah
Williams, Sharon, vice president,

Teenage Choir

Corker, Gregory
Dyson, Felicia
Dyson, Marvin
Edwards, Arita
Huggins, Kirk
Huggins, Sharon
Langston, Charles
McCray, Anita
McCrary, Alex
McCrary, Averil
McCrary, Corlis
McCrary, Darold
McCrary, Denise
McCrary, LaVoris
Moorehead, Wynette
Ponder, Anita
Simmons, Julius
Smith, Jackie
Talton, Chauncil
Talton, Karen
Talton, Kathy

1985

Youth Choir

Bellamy, Donnita
Daniely, Andrena
Demons, Jamehl
Ellison, Jeffery
Giles, Melissa
Palmer, Felice
Palmer, Tomia
Ponder, Celeste
Ponder Keisa
Smith, Erica
Talton, Belinda
Taylor, Tonja
Weatherspoon, Katina

1988

Chancel Choir

Abrams, Linda
Brewton, Philip
Cleveland, Marie Taylor
Daniely, Barbara
Demons, Jacquelyn
Gadsden, Ada
Giles, Hope
Huff, Jeanette
Junior, Jr., E. J.
Kimbro, Lillian
Langston, Wilmetta
Lavender, Doris
Marshall, Mary
McCray, Evelyn

Nelson, Addie
Palmer, Thomas
Smith, Evelyn
Street, Gloria
Taylor, John
Weatherspoon, Brenda, director
Weatherspoon, Elijah

Young People's Choir

Bellamy, Donnita
Brewton, Kristy
Burton, Lesli
Burton, Lori
Conteh, Alfred
Conteh, Alvin
Giles, Melissa
McRae, Ernest
McRae, Michele
Magee, Audrey, director
Palmer, Felice
Palmer, Tomia
Ponder, Celeste
Smith, Erica
Street, Dexter
Street, Gregory
Taylor, Victor
Walker, Daphne
Weatherspoon, Genard
Weatherspoon, Katina

Children's Choir

Brenda Weatherspoon, director
Collins, David
Collins, Kimberly

Giles, Arnold
Johnson, Jesica
Magee, Candice
Magee, Darian
Nelson, Cynara
Singh, Alya
Taylor, Tiffany
Turner, Darius
Turner, Marquis
Walker, Melanie
Weatherspoon, Kerey

1991

Abrams, Linda
Brewton, Phillip
Cleveland, Marie
Daniely, Barbara
Demons, Jacquelyn
Gadsden, Ada
Giles, Hope
Huff, Jeanette
Junior, Jr., E. J.
Kimbro, Lillian
Langston, Wilmetta
Lavender, Doris
Magee, Audrey, organist
Marshall, Mary J.
McCray, Evelyn
Nelson, Addie
Palmer, Thomas
Smith, Evelyn
Street, Gloria
Taylor, John
Turner, Mattie

Weatherspoon, Brenda, director of music
Weatherspoon, Elijah
Williams, Cheryl

1994

Brewton, Philip
Cleveland, Marie Taylor
Daniely, Barbara
Demons, Jacquelyn
Dickerson, Cheryl, secretary
Gadsden, Ada
Giles, Hope, vice president
Harris, Gloria Street, assistant secretary
Huff, Jeanette K.
Jackson, Wilmetta L.
Junior, Jr., E. J.
Kimbro, Lillian, Treasurer
Lavender, Doris
Magee, Audrey
Marshall, Mary J.
McCray, Evelyn, president
Nelson, Addie
Palmer, Thomas J.
Smith, Evelyn
Taylor, John, chaplain
Turner, Mattie
Weatherspoon, Brenda, director
Weatherspoon, Elijah

1995

Brewton, Philip
Daniely, Barbara
Demons, Jacqueline

Dickerson, Cheryl
Gadsden, Ada
Giles, Hope
Harris, Gloria Street
Huff, Jeanette K.
Jackson, Wilmetta L.
Junior, Jr., E. J.
Kimbro, Lillian
Lavender, Doris
Magee, Audrey, organist
Marshall, Mary J.
McCray, Evelyn
Nelson, Addie
Palmer, Thomas J.
Smith, Evelyn
Taylor, John, chaplain
Turner, Mattie
Weatherspoon, Brenda, minister of music
Weatherspoon, Elijah

1996

Brewton, Philip
Daniely, Barbara
Demons, Jacquelyn
Dickerson, Cheryl
Gadsden, Ada
Giles, Hope
Harris, Gloria S
Huff, Jeanette K.
Jackson, Wilmetta L.
Junior, Jr., E. J.
Kimbro, Lillian
Lavender, Doris

Marshall, Mary J.
McCray, Evelyn
Moorehead, Willie D., pianist
Nelson, Addie
Palmer, Thomas J.
Prater, Jacqueline, organist
Smith, Evelyn
Taylor, John, chaplain
Turner, Mattie
Weatherspoon, Brenda, minister of music
Weatherspoon, Elijah

1997

Brewton, Philip
Daniely, Barbara
Demons, Jacquelyn
Dickerson, Cheryl
Gadsden, Ada
Giles, Hope
Harris, Gloria Street
Huff, Jeanette K.
Jackson, Wilmetta L.
Junior, Jr., E. J.
Kimbro, Lillian
Lavender, Doris
Marshall, Mary J.
McCray, Evelyn
Palmer, Thomas J.
Smith, Evelyn
Taylor, John, chaplain
Turner, Mattie
Weatherspoon, Brenda, minister of music
Weatherspoon, Elijah

1998

Brewton, Philip
Daniely, Barbara, secretary
Demons, Jacqueline
Dickerson, Cheryl
Gadsden, Ada
Giles, Hope
Harris, Gloria Street, president
Huff, Jeanette K., vice president
Jackson, Wilmetta L.
Junior, Jr., E. J.
Kimbro, Lillian, treasurer
Lavender, Doris
McCray, Evelyn
Marshall, Mary J., chaplain
Moorehead, Willie D., organist
Nelson, Addie
Palmer, Thomas J.
Smith, Evelyn
Taylor, John
Turner, Mattie
Weatherspoon, Brenda, minister of
music
Weatherspoon, Elijah

2000

Brewton, Philip
Daniely, Barbara, secretary
Demons, Jacquelyn S.
Dickerson Cheryl
Gadsden, Ada M.
Giles, Hope
Harris, Gloria Street, president
Huff, Jeanette K., vice president

Jackson, Wilmetta S. L.
Kimbro, Lillian D., treasurer
Marshall, Mary J., chaplin
McCray, Evelyn D.
Moorehead, Willie D., organist
Palmer, Thomas J.
Smith, Evelyn
Taylor, John, Jr.
Weatherspoon, Brenda, minister of
music
Weatherspoon, Elijah

2005

Julius C. Simmons Gospel Choir

Abrams, Jessica
Abrams, Linda
Barrett, Jenita
Bellamy, Donnita
Brewton, Philip
Corker, Grace
Croom, Christopher
Crumbly, Dorothy
Colvard, Bridget
Cruven, Nexis
Daniely, Barbara
Dickerson, Cheryl
Edwards, Mary
Foster, Willie
Giles, Hope
Harris, Gloria Street
Hogan, Anita
Hogan, Timothy
Huff, Jeanette
Jackson, Wilmetta L.

Kenney, JaShondra
Marshall, Mary Julia
Nelson, Addie
Palmer, Barbara
Palmer, Corey
Palmer, Thomas

Singh, Faye
Turner, Mattie R.
Weatherspoon, Brenda
Weatherspoon, Elijah
West, Geneva

Christmas Cantata Roster

1977

Ballard, Phil
Brewton, Phillip
Demons, Jacquelyn
Gadsden, Ada
Garrard, Reginald
Hicks, Murlennum
Kimbro, Lillian
Langston, Wilmetta
McCray, Evelyn
Mathis, Alice
Marshall Mary J.
Moorehead, W. D., accompanying at organ and piano
Palmer, Thomas
Sampson, Gladyce, president
Street, Gloria
Taylor, Marie
Taylor, John
Weatherspoon, Elijah
Weatherspoon, Brenda
Weldon, Annie

1980

Brewton, Phillip
Cleveland, Marie
Demons, Jacquelyn
Gadsden, Ada M.
Garrard, Reginald
Hardee, Wyonnie
Harris, James
Jowers, George

Kimbro, Lillian
Konan, Jacqueline
Langston, Wilmetta
Lewis, Faye
Lindsey, Randolph
Marshall, Mary J.
Mathis, Alice
Mathis, William S.
Miller, Joselyn
Moultrie, William
Palmer, Thomas J.
Rice, Doris
Sampson, Ulysses T.
Simmons, Martha
Street, Gloria
Taylor, John
Turner, Mattie R.
Weatherspoon, Brenda S.
Weatherspoon, Elijah
Weldon, Annie K.
Williams, Robert

1981

Brewton, Phillip
Cleveland, Marie
Demons, Jacquelyn
Dickerson, Cheryl
Ellis, III, Alfred
Fobbs, Darrell
Freeman, Woody
Gadsden, Ada M.
Garrard, Reginald
Hardee, Wyonnie

Harris, James
Homer, Sharon
Jowers, George, Jr.
Langston, Wilmetta
Marshall, Mary J.
Mathis, Alice
McCray, Evelyn
Palmer, Thomas J.
Rice, Doris
Simmons, Martha
Street, Gloria
Stripling, Greg
Taylor, John
Turner, Mattie R.
Weatherspoon, Brenda S.
Weatherspoon, Elijah
Weldon, Annie K.
Willingham, Betty S.

1982

Adams, George, brass ensemble
Allred, Angela
Barnette, Thomas
Brewton, Phillip
Cleveland, Marie
Demons, Jacquelyn
Dickerson, Cheryl
Fronz, Howard
Gadsden, Ada M.
Gerrard, Reginald
Hardee, Wyonnie
Harris, James, accompanying at piano
and organ
Jackson, James
Jowers, George Jr.

Lanston, Wilmetta S.
Marshall, Mary J.
Mathis, Alice
McCray, Evelyn
Miller, Heidi
Miller, Joselyn
Moore, Clarence W.
Moultrie, William
Palmer, Barbara
Palmer, Thomas J.
Ragin, Trelvis
Randolph, Lindsey, brass ensemble
Rice, Doris
Simmons, Martha
Street, Gloria B.
Stripling, Greg, accompanying at piano
and organ
Taylor, John
Walker, Diane E.
Weatherspoon, Brenda S., director
Weatherspoon, Elijah
Wells, Tina
White, Elizabeth
Willingham, Betty S.

1983

Abrams, Jessica
Brewton, Phillip
Demons, Jacquelyn
Dickerson, Cheryl
Ellis, III, Alfred
Gadsden, Ada M.
Giles, Hope B.
Harris, Gloria
Jackson, James

Jackson, Wilmetta S.
Junior, Jr., E. J.
Kimbro, Lillian
McCray, Evelyn
Magee, Audrey
Marshall, Mary J.
Miller-Jackson, Joselyn
Moore, Clarence W.
Moultrie, William
Nelson, Addie
Oglesby, Gus
Prater, Jacqueline
Rice, Doris
Strong, Faye
Taylor, John
Turner, Mattie R.
Weatherspoon, Brenda S.
Weatherspoon, Elijah
Weatherspoon, Katina
White, Elizabeth
Williams, Barbara
Williams, Jimmy L.

1984

Adkins, Joseph
Bellamy, Donna D.
Brewton, Philip
Cleveland, Marie
Demons, Jacquelyn
Demons, Jamehl
Dickerson, Cheryl
Ellis, III, Alfred
Gadsden, Ada M.
Hardee, Wyonnie
Harris, James

Kimbro, Lillian D.
Langston, Wilmetta S.
Lewis, Faye
Lindsey, Randolph
McCray, Evelyn
McGee, Edward
Magee, Audrey
Marshall, Mary J.
Moore, Clarence W.
Moultrie, William
Palmer, Thomas J.
Simmons, Martha
Smith, Evelyn
Street, Gloria
Taylor, John
Walker, Diane
Weatherspoon, Brenda
Weatherspoon, Elijah
White, Elizabeth
Willingham, Betty S.

1985

Brewton, Phillip
Cleveland, Marie
Daniely, Barbara
Demons, Jacquelyn
Dickerson, Cheryl
Freeman, Woody
Gadsden, Ada M.
Hardee, Wyonnie
Harleston, Vernon
Harris, James
Jackson, James
Jackson, Joycelyn
Junior, Jr., E. J.

Kimbro, Lillian
Langston, Wilmetta S.
Lewis, Faye
Lindsey, Randolph
McCray, Evelyn D.
Magee, Audrey
Marshall, Mary J.
Martin, Clara
Moore, Clarence
Moultrie, William
Nelson, Addie
Palmer, Thomas J.
Rice, Doris
Simmons, Martha
Street, Gloria
Taylor, John
Walker, Diane E.
Walker, Jeraldine
Weatherspoon, Brenda S.
Weatherspoon, Elijah
White, Elizabeth
Williams, David

Cantata Youth Choir

Bellamy, Donnita
Daniely, Andrena
Demons, Jamehl
Ellison, Jeffery
Giles, Melissa
Palmer, Felice
Palmer, Tomia
Ponder, Celeste
Ponder, Keisha
Smith, Erica
Talton, Belinda

Taylor, Tonja
Weatherspoon, Katina

1986

Brewton, Phillip
Cleveland, Marie
Daniely, Andrena
Demons, Jacquelyn
Demons, Jamehl L.
Dickerson, Cheryl
Ellis, Alfred III.
Gadsden, Ada M.
Hardee, Wyonnie
Harris, James
Jackson, Birdelle
Jackson, James
Jackson, Joycelyn
Junior, Jr., E. J.
Kimbro, Lillian
Langston, Wilmetta
Lewis, Faye
Lindsey, Randolph
McCray, Evelyn D.
Magee, Audrey
Marshall, Mary J.
Moore, Clarence
Moultrie, William
Nelson, Addie
Palmer, Thomas J.
Rice, Doris
Simmons, Martha
Street, Gloria
Taylor, John
Weatherspoon, Brenda S.
Weatherspoon, Elijah

White, Elizabeth
Williams, Jimmie L.

Cantata's Young Musicians

Brewton, Kristy
Burton, Leslie
Burton, Lori
Conteh, Alfred
Conteh, Alvin
McRae, Michele
Palmer, Felice
Palmer, Tomia
Simmons, Paron J.
Smith, Erica
Taylor, Victor
Walker, Daphnye
Weatherspoon, Katina

1989

Brewton, Phillip
Brown, Sedric
Cleveland, Marie
Daniely, Barbara
Demons, Jacquelyn
Frazier, Fred
Gadsden, Ada M.
Giles, Hope
Huff, Jeanette K.
Jackson, James
Junior, Jr., E. J.
Kimbro, Lillian
Langston, Wilmetta
Lavender, Doris
McCray, Evelyn D.

Magee, Audrey
Marshall, Mary J.
Moultrie, William
Nelson, Addie
Rice, Doris
Street, Gloria
Taylor, John
Weatherspoon, Brenda S.
Weatherspoon, Elijah
White, Elizabeth

Children's Choir

Giles, Arnold
Magee, Candice
Magee, Darian
Nelson, Cynara
Weatherspoon, Kerey

Youth Choir

Brewton, Kristy
Daniely, Andrena
Giles, Melissa
Lucas, Willanda
Palmer, Felice
Palmer, Tomia
Walker, Turkessa
Weatherspoon, Katina

1990

Brewton, Philip
Cleveland, Marie
Daniely, Barbara
Demons, Jacquelyn

Dickerson, Cheryl
Gadsden, Ada M.
Giles, Hope
Huff, Jeanette
Jackson, James
Jackson, Birdelle
Kimbro, Lillian
Langston, Wilmetta
Lavender, Doris
Lindsey, Randolph
Marshall, Mary J.
McCray, Evelyn
Miller-Jackson, Joselyn
Moultrie, William
Nelson, Addie
Palmer, Thomas
Rice, Doris
Street, Gloria
Taylor, John
Weatherspoon, Brenda
Weatherspoon, Elijah
White, Elizabeth

Children's Choir

Giles, Arnold
Jarris, Natasha
Jackson, Alvontee
Johnson, Jessica
Magee, Candice
Magee, Darian
Nelson, Cynara
Taylor, Tiffany
Weatherspoon, Kerey

Youth Choir

Abrams, Jessica
Fluellen, Meaza
Giles, Melissa
Hughley, JoVonn
Palmer, Felice
Street, Greg
Weatherspoon, Katina

1991

Abrams, Emily K.
Brewton, Philip
Cleveland, Marie
Daniely, Barbara
Demons, Jacquelyn
Dickerson, Cheryl
Gadsden, Ada M.
Giles, Hope
Guy, Andrea L.
Herbert, Robin
Huff, Jeanette
Jackson, James
Miller-Jackson, Joselyn
Jackson, Wilmetta S.
Junior, Jr., E. J.
Kimbro, Lillian
Lavender, Doris
Lindsey, Randolph
McCray, Evelyn
Magee, Audrey
Marshall, Mary J.
Massey, Mark
Moore, Clarence W.
Moultrie, William
Nelson, Addie
Palmer, Thomas, J.

Pitts, Tina
Prater, Jacqueline
Rice, Doris
Street, Gloria
Taylor, John
Turner, Mattie R.
Weatherspoon, Brenda
Weatherspoon, Elijah
Weatherspoon, Katina
White, Elizabeth
Williams, Barbara
Williams, Jimmie L.

Youth Choir

Abrams, Jessica
Fluellen, Meaza
Giles, Melissa
Magee, Candice
Oates, Patrice
Oates, Rhonda
Oates, Wanda
Palmer, Felice
Taylor, Tiffany
Udoh, Imo

1992

Brewton, Phillip
Cleveland, Marie
Corker, Grace
Crooks, Kenneth
Daniely, Barbara
Demons, Jacquelyn
Dickerson, Cheryl
Gadsden, Ada M.

Giles, Hope
Harris, Gloria
Huff, Jeanette
Jackson, James
Junior, Jr., E. J.
Kimbro, Lillian
King, Randy
Langston, Wilmetta
Lavender, Doris
McCray, Evelyn
Magee, Audrey
Marshall, Mary J.
Miller, Jackson, Joselyn
Moore, Clarence
Nelson, Addie
Prater, Jacqueline
Rice, Doris
Simmons, Martha
Slusser, Dean
Smith, Evelyn
Strong, Faye Lewis
Taylor, John
Turner, Mattie R.
Weatherspoon, Brenda S.
Weatherspoon, Elijah
White, Elizabeth
Williams, Barbara
Williams, Jimmy L.

1995

Brewton, Phillip
Corker, Grace
Crooks, Kenneth
Daniely, Barbara
Demons, Jacquelyn

Dickerson, Cheryl
Gadsden, Ada M.
Giles, Hope
Harris, Gloria S.
Huff, Jeanette K.
Jackson, James
Jackson, Wilmetta L.
Kimbro, Lillian
McCray, Evelyn
Magee, Audrey
Marshall, Mary J.
Miller, Jackson, Joselyn
Moore, Clarence
Moultrie, William
Nelson, Addie
Oglesby, Gus
Rice, Doris
Taylor, Katina W.
Taylor, John
Turner, Mattie R.
Weatherspoon, Brenda S.
Weatherspoon, Elijah
White, Elizabeth

Harmonic Tones

Abrams, Jessica
Giles, Arnold
Magee, Candice
Magee, Darian
Mathis, Richard Allen
Nelson, Cynara
Taylor, Tiffany
Turner, Marquis
Walker, Sabastain
Weatherspoon, Kerey

1996

Booker, Lennox
Brewton, Phillip
Corker, Grace
Crooks, Kenneth
Daniely, Barbara
Demons, Jacquelyn
Dickerson, Cheryl
Duffie, Mack
Gadsden, Ada M.
Giles, Hope
Harris, Gloria
Huff, Jeanette K.
Jackson, James
Jackson, Wilmetta S. L.
Junior, Jr., E. J.
Kimbro, Lillian
King, Randy
McCray, Evelyn
Magee, Audrey
Marshall, Mary J.
Miller, Jackson, Joselyn
Moultrie, William
Oglesby, Gus
Palmer, Thomas J.
Rice, Doris
Strong, Faye Lewis
Taylor, John
Taylor, Katina W.
Taylor, Tiffany
Mattie Turner
Walker, Sabastain
Weatherspoon, Brenda S.
Weatherspoon, Elijah
White, Elizabeth

Williams, Barbara

1998

Brewton, Phillip
Daniely, Barbara
Demons, Jacquelyn
Dickerson, Cheryl
Gadsden, Ada M.
Giles, Hope
Harris, Gloria
Huff, Jeanette K.
Jackson, James
Jackson, Wilmetta L.
Kimbro, Lillian
King, Randy
McCray, Evelyn
Marshall, Mary J.
Miller, Jackson, Joselyn
Moorehead, Willie D.
Moultrie, William
Nelson, Addie
Oglesby, Gus
Palmer, Thomas J
Rice, Doris
Smith, Evelyn
Strong, Faye Lewis
Taylor, John
Taylor, Katina W.
Turner, Pamela
Weatherspoon, Brenda S.
Weatherspoon, Elijah
White, Elizabeth
Williams, Barbara

2003

Ballard, Danielle
Banks, Pamela
Boyer, Faye
Brewton, Kristy
Brewton, Phillip
Carson, Mary
Corker, Grace
Crumbly, Dorothy
Daniels, Dwayne
Daniely, Barbara
Edwards, Mary J.
Gadsden, Ada M.
Giles, Hope
Green, Quinton
Harris, Gloria S.
Hogan, Anita M.
Huff, Jeanette
Jackson, James
Jackson, Wilmetta L.
Kimbro, Lillian
McCray, Evelyn
McSee, Wilmetta S.L.
Miller, Jackson, Joselyn
Moore, Gregory
Moultrie, William
Nelson, Addie
Nicholson, Donnie
Oglesby, Gus
Palmer, Barbara
Palmer, Thomas, J.
Palmer, Tomia E.
Rice, Doris
Smith, Evelyn
Taylor, John

Weatherspoon, Brenda S.
Weatherspoon, Elijah
White, Elizabeth

2004

Ballard, Danielle
Banks, Pamela
Brewton, Phillip
Carson, Mary
Crumbly, Dorothy
Daniels, Dwayne
Daniely, Barbara
Edwards, Mary J.
Gadsden, Ada M.
Giles, Hope
Giles, Melissa
Green, Quinton
Hogan, Anita M.
Huff, Jeanette
Jackson, James
Johnson, Jamie
Kimbro, Lillian
McCray, Evelyn
McSee, Wilmetta S. L.
Miller-Jackson, Joselyn
Nicholson, Donnie
Oglesby, Gus
Palmer, Thomas, J.
Rice, Doris
Smith, Evelyn
Taylor, John
Turner, Mattie R.
Weatherspoon, Brenda S.
Weatherspoon, Elijah
Weatherspoon, Katina R.

White, Elizabeth
Williams, Barbara

2005

Abrams, Jessica
Ballard, Danielle
Banks, Pamela
Boyer, Faye L. S.
Brewton, Phillip
Crumbly, Dorothy M.
Daniely, Barbara
Gadsden, Ada M.
Giles, Hope
Giles, Melissa
Harris, Gloria
Hogan, Anita M.
Jackson, James
Johnson, Jamie
Kimbro, Lillian
McCray, Evelyn D.
McSee, Wilmetta
Marshall, Mary J.
Miller-Jackson, Joselyn
Moultrie, William
Oglesby, Gus
Palmer, Thomas, J.
Rice, Doris
Weatherspoon, Brenda S.
Weatherspoon, Elijah
Weatherspoon, Katina R.
White, Elizabeth
Williams, Barbara

2008

Abrams, Jessica
Ballard, Danielle
Banks, Pamela
Boyer, Faye L. S.
Brewton, Phillip
Carson, Mary
Coar, Janya
Corker, Grace
Crooks, Kenneth
Crumbly, Dorothy
Daniely, Barbara
Daniely, Sylvia
Davis, Jarvis
Edwards, Mary
Giles, Hope
Gore, LaWanda
Green, Quintin
Harris, Gloria
Huff, Jeanette K.
Johnson, Jamie
Johnson, Melissa
Kendrick, Katina
Kendrick, Karen
Kenney, Kristy
King, Randy
Lindsey, Mildred
McSee, Wilmetta L. J.
Moultrie, William
Nicholson, Donnie
Oglesby, Gus
Rice, Doris
Smith, Frank
Taylor, John
Turner, Glyn

Weatherspoon, Brenda S.
Weatherspoon, Elijah
White, Elizabeth
Williams, Barbara

2011

Abrams, Jessica
Banks, Pamela
Coar, Janza
Crumbly, Dorothy
Crumbly, Morgan
Cruver, Neris
Daniely, Barbara
Daniely, Sylvia
Edwards, Mary
Fobbs, Darrell
Fobbs, Garfield
Fobbs, Rosa
Foster, Willie
Gibson, Darion
Giles, Hope
Giles, Leonard
Huff, Jeanette
Jackson, AlDevin
Jackson, Birdell
Johnson, Bishop Jamie
Jordan, Antwan
Kenney, Kristy
Kerr, David
Langston, Wilmetta McSee
Lindsey, Mildred
Lindsey, Randolph
Moore, Reverend Gregory E.
Moore, Helen-Louise
Moore, Mary Grace

Nelson, Addie
Rice, Doris
Taylor, Eric
Thompson, Ruth
Weatherspoon, Brenda
Weatherspoon, Kerey
White, Elizabeth
Williams, Barbara
Wilson, Keith

2013

Abrams, Jessica
Banks, Pam
Beaver, Kierra
Brown, Kira
Carter, Brittney
Daniely, Barbara
Dawson, Sidra
Edwards, Mary
Ellis, III, Alfred
Giles, Hope
Giles, Leonard
Gore, Lawanda
Howard, Jasmin
Huff, Jeanette
Jackson, AlDevin
Jackson, Alvonetee
Jackson, Birdell
Johnson, Bishop Jamie
Kendrick, Jessica

Kenney, Kristy
Kerr, David
Lindsey, Mildred
Lindsey, Randolph
Marshall, Quan
Moore, Mary Grace
Moore, Reverend Gregory
Moore, William
Moorehead, Douglas
Nelson, Addie
Nelson, Cynara
Oglesby, Reverend Gus
Rembert, Curtis
Rice, Doris
Robinson, Thomas
Thomas, Joseph
Thompson, Ruth
Weatherspoon, Brenda
Weatherspoon, Kerey
White, Elizabeth
Williams, Barbara
Williams, Edwin
Wilson, Keith
Wright, Breona
Wynn, Jason

Ushers Ministry

Officers and Roster

Allen, Lee Clara
Appling, Oliver
Baldwin, Mattie Mathis
Baldwin, Ransom
Beauford, Samuel
Boyer, Jeanette
Brinson, Elizabeth
Brown, Willie
Crumbly, Dorothy
Crumbly, Issac
Daniely, Clarence
Davis, Earnest
Davis, Johnny C.
Davis, Lessie
Dean, Charlie Mae, president
Dean, Clemont
Dean, Loistine Smith
Dent, Annie
Duffie, Ruby
Duffie, Mack
Eaton, Bernice
Edwards, Andrew
Edwards, Mary
Emanuel, Annie
Evans, Rosa
Hand, Bernice
Harris, Lillie Mae
Hiley, Irene
Hollinshed, Dorothy
Hollinshed, Hennie Robinson
Hollinshed, Leon
Hollinshed, Mae Alice

Horton, Dollie
Huggins, Mary
Jackson, Lonnie
Jenkins, Joyce
Jennings, Mary
Jessie, Inez Smith
Jordan, Freddie
Jordan, Mattie Kate Marshall
Little, Lila
Lockett, Kathy
Mathis, Jewel
McCrary, Averil
McCrary, Felma
McCrary, J.D.
McCrary, Luetta
McCrary, Ronald
McRae, Ernest
McRae, Lorine
Maddox, Ida
Meadows, Diane
Miller, Carrie
Morgan, James
Moorehead, W. Douglas
Nix, Lillian
Pearson, Rochelle
Reed, John
Rouse, Edith
Rouse, Louise
Sanders, Louise
Simmons, Alma
Singh, Faye
Small, Denise
Smith, Alfred L.

Smith, Lewis T.

Smith, Amos

Stallworth, Houston

Talton, Money Mae, president, 1978, president emeritus, 1999

Taylor, Delia

Towns, Delia

Towns, Elia

Turner, Karen

Underwood, Pearlie Mae

Wells, Eddie

Wilcox, Sandra

Wilkerson, Annie P.

Young, R. C.

Teenage Ushers

1978

Burns, Jolita

Cornelious, Dwight

Eaton, Darryl

Eaton, David

Eaton, Deidre

Hand, Beverly

Hand, Sidney

Horton, Alrae

Horton, Roderick

Huggins, Kirk

Johnson, Celestine

Jordan, Felecia

Jordan, Phillip

Langston, Charles III

Mathis, Opie

Mathis, Roni

McCoy, Rosie Lee Emanuel

McCrary, Alex

McCrary, Averil

McCrary, Darold

McCrary, Denise

McCrary, Gerald

Moody, Ronnie

Morgan, Duncan

Morgan, Shelia

Plant, Shavonda

Ponder, Anita

Simmons, Julius C. Jr.

Talton, Karen

Talton, Kathy

Taylor, John III

Wilkerson, Angela

Williams, Angeline

Sponsors:

Wilmetta Langston

Barbara Daniely

Amos Smith

Katye Murphy Troup Ushers

1978

Bellamy, Donnita

Brewton, Kristy

Brewton, Phyllis

Daniely, Andrena

Demons, Jamehl

Mangrum, Kimberly

Moorehead, Lynnette

Palmer, Tomia

Palmer, Felicia

Singh, Millicent
Smith, Erica
Street, Dexter
Taylor, Tonya
Weatherspoon, Genard
Weatherspoon, Katina

Sponsors:

Inez Brewton
Annie P. Wilkerson

Children's Ushers

Daniely, Larry
Durham, Katherine
Edwards, Alfred
Edwards, Andrew
Edwards, Cassandra
Edwards, Diane
Marshall, Karen
Martin, Barbara Ann
McCray, Jacquelyn
McCray, Paulette

Ambassador Ushers

1978

Cornelious, Dwight
Langston, Charles
McCrary Averil
Morgan, Duncan
Huggins, Kirk
Jordon, Philip
McCrary, Alex

McCrary, Jerry
Moody, Ronnie
Simmons, Julius Jr.
Taylor, John III
Advisor: Amos Smith

Katye Murphy Troup Ushers

1980

Bellamy, Donnita
Brewton, Kristy
Brewton, Phyllis
Daniely, Andrena
Demons, Jemahl
Mangrum, Kimberly,
Mangrum, Perry
Moorehead, Lynette
Singh, Millicent
Smith, Erica
Street, Dexter
Taylor, Tonya
Weatherspoon, Gernard
Weatherspoon, Katina

Sponsors:

Inez Brewton
Annie P. Wilkerson

Teenage Ushers

1980

Eaton, Darryl
Eaton, Deidre

Hand, Beverly
Hand, Sidney
Horton, Alre
Horton, Roderick
Huggins, Kirk
Johnson, Celestine
Jordan, Felicia
Jordan, Phillip
Langston, III, Charles N.
McCrary, Alex
McCrary, Averil

McCrary, Jerry
Mathis, Opie
Moody, Ronnie
Morgan, Shelia
Simmons, Julius C.
Taylor, John III
Wilkerson, Angela

RESOURCES

Books

1. Bellamy, Donnie. *The History of Shiloh Baptist Church.* 1999. Virginia: The Donning Company.
2. Foner, Eric. *Reconstruction: America's Unfinished Revolution, 1863–1877.* 1988. New York: HarperCollins Publishers Inc.
3. Johnson, Alonzo and Paul Jersild, eds. *Ain't Gonna Lay My 'Ligion Down.* 1996. Columbia: University of South Carolina Press.
4. Troup, Cornelius V. *Distinguished Negro Georgians.* 1962. Dallas: Royal Publishing Company.
5. Wagner, Clarence M. *Profiles of Black Georgia Baptist: 206 Years of Georgia Baptist and 100 Years of National Baptist History.* Atlanta: Bennett Brothers Printing Company.

Journals

6. Butts, Cora L. *"Dr. W. T. Ford, class of 1913 died."* Fort Valley State College Peachite, vol. 5, issue 3, (December 1946), p.8.
7. *"College Speakers, 1946-1947."* Fort Valley State College Bulletin, vol. 8, no. 4. (May 1947). p. 105
8. Green, Jan. *"Protesters Stop in Fort Valley."* Fort Valley State College Peachite. May 1970.
9. *"Reporting the News of the Month."* Fort Valley State College Bulletins. (May 1949). p.5.

Newspaper Articles

10. *"Black Man [W. S. M. Banks] Seeks Fort Valley City Post," Macon Telegraph,* 5 Feb 1964.

11. "Chisholm Speaks, What Do You People Want Now*?" Macon Telegraph,* 8 July 1976.

12. "Fort Valley Elects First Black Mayor." *Macon Telegraph,* 4 Apr. 1980.

13. "Fort Valley Rights Group Reaches Accord with Revco, Ends Picketing." *Macon Telegraph,* 4 Dec 1983.

14. "Local Blacks See Ruling As Setback." *Macon Telegraph,* 29 June 1978.

15. "Negro (Benjamin S. Anderson) Leads Fort Valley Council Race." *Macon Telegraph,* 4 Apr 1968.

16. "Negro Ministers To Attend Course: State Body of White Churches to Sponsor Insitute [Fort Valley]." *Macon Telegraph,* 10 May 1940.

17. "Peach Election Law Challenge: Suit Depends On U.S. Action." *Macon Telegraph,* 27 Jun 1978.

18. "Picketing Costly To Peach County (Shoplifting Case) Revco Drugs." *Macon Telegraph,* 20 Oct 1983.

19. "Race For Mayor Highlight of Fort Valley Vote Today." *Macon Telegraph,* 23 Mar 1960.

20. "Revco Becomes Target Of Black Boycott." *Leader Tribune,* 21 Jul 1983.

21. "Revco Confrontation Charges To Be Dropped But Picketing To Continue." *Macon Telegraph,* 1 Dec 1983.

22. "Rudolph Carson to be Sworn in as Fort Valley's Mayor, April 17." *Leader Tribune,* 10 April 1980.

23. "SCLC to hunt hiring bias." *Macon Telegraph,* 16 June 1978..

24. "Second Black Man (AJ Edwards) is Candidate For Office In Fort Valley." *Macon Telegraph,* February 26, 1964.

25. Powell, Billy. "Trinity Baptist." *Leader Tribune,* 7 Oct 1976.

Archives and Manuscripts

26. Arnold, Angeola, "Trinity as I Knew It," a paper, unpublished. Fort Valley.
27. Bond, Horace Mann, "Horace Mann Bond papers, 1939–1945," H. A. Hunt Memorial Library, Heritage Collection. Fort Valley, Georgia: Fort Valley State College.
28. Citizenship Education Commission, Citizenship Education Commission miscellaneous papers, unpublished.
29. Julius C. Simmons Collection, 1958–1999. (Sermons, programs, etc.) Trinity Missionary Baptist Church Archives, Fort Valley, Georgia: Trinity Missionary Baptist Church.

Documents

30. Ancestry.com. 1910 United States Federal Census. [database on-line]. Provo, UT, USA: Ancestry.com Operation Inc., 2006.
31. Ancestry.com. 1920 United States Federal Census.[database on-line] Provo, UT, USA: Ancestry.com Operation Inc., 2010.
32. Ancestry.com. 1930 United States Federal Census. [database on-line]. Provo, UT, USA: Ancestry.com Operation Inc., 2002.

1912 TRINITY 1980
YESTERDAY, TODAY AND TOMORROW

Photo By
Isaac Smith, Jr.

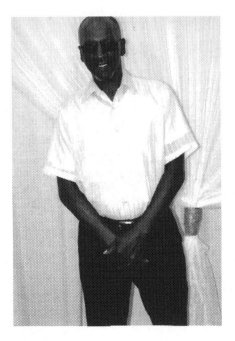